Fit for Rugby

Bev Risman

General Editor   Peter Verney
Medical Adviser   Dr Alan Maryon-Davis
                    MB, Bchir, MSc, MRCP, MFCM
                    Medical Officer
                    Health Education Council

B T Batsford Ltd · London

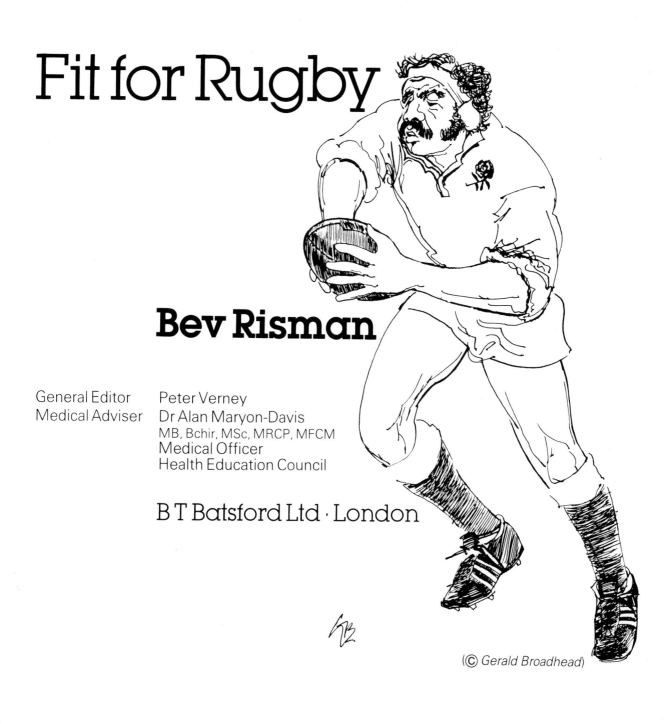

ISBN 0 7134 4243 3

Typeset by Tek-Art Ltd, Kent
and printed in Great Britain by
R J Acford
Chichester, Sussex
for the publishers
B.T. Batsford Ltd.
4 Fitzhardinge Street
London W1H 0AH

Contents

Foreword

If there is one thing certain in this transient world it is that as our working days get shorter, and sometimes fewer in face of technological advance, we shall be 'burdened' by more and more leisure time. Some of us will occupy ourselves in sedentary occupations, but many more will prefer to take more and regular exercise – and this will often mean *devoting greater time and effort to sport.*

These books are not written with the beginner in mind – although he or she will find much of value in these pages – but they are rather designed for the enthusiastic amateur; the committed sportsman or sportswoman, someone who has tasted, experienced and enjoyed their sport and who wishes to improve their performance and consequently gain greater enjoyment from it.

The twin pillars of improvement in any occupation are experience and skill. Experience can only come with time and a long association with the sport, but skill in any sport is dependent on, and in many cases the product of, fitness. A general degree of fitness – physical and mental – is required in the first place to act as a foundation for the subsequent developed and specialised fitness which is needed by the enthusiast. It is the purpose of this series of books, written by acknowledged experts of great experience, to help achieve this specific fitness.

Section I will be of general interest in terms of testing and establishing basic fitness, and will be of some value to absolute beginners wishing to make a start in the game of rugby. Section II concentrates on the specific needs and related aspects – equipment, training, competition advice, etc. – of rugby, and how to attain fitness in rugby. Section III deals with the medical aspects of the sport – the injuries and conditions associated with rugby and, finally, some First Aid principles, aimed primarily at emergencies which might occur on the sports field, but which will be of use to anyone under any circumstances.

SECTION 1
General Fitness

The Fitness Ethic

One of the most significant trends in everyday living over the past thirty years has been a growing interest in fitness. Books on general fitness abound, and most incorporate an analysis of the need for fitness, the effect of fitness on the human body and the beneficial effect when that body is fit. Although this series is designed with specific sports in mind, there is no doubt that a general degree of fitness is of inestimable value to the sportsman or sportwoman, especially as more and more people are coming into sport at a later age.

The doctors declare that there is a close link between physical fitness and mental alertness, and that a fit person, taking regular exercise, is better able to face the pace and rigours, and the emotional and physical stresses of day-to-day living. He is also more likely to sleep well and feel well. More particularly, a fit body is an efficient body.

In addition, although fitness is not a passport to health, it does make you less liable to sickness and more able to effect a speedy recovery from illness. Of great value in the field of sport is the fact that a fit person tires less easily than someone who is not, and injury in sport is often directly caused by fatigue.

The doctors will also tell you that the fit have stronger hearts, and regular exercise reduces the risk of heart disease; moreover, that lack of exercise is a major cause of heart disease, and that, if you do have a heart attack, you will have a better chance of surviving it if you are fit.

For those participating in sport, fitness gives you confidence that you won't crack up halfway, makes muscle fatigue, pulls and other injuries less likely, and gives you a competitive edge.

Fit for Sport?

Most people are fit enough for most sports and games played at a gentle pace. However, there is a basic assumption behind this series that the reader is proposing to play his sport more regularly and at a greater intensity than hitherto – in short, the committed sportsman. So certain medical warnings are necessary, and a medical check-up is advisable beforehand.

This is particularly important for anyone over 35, especially if taking up strenuous sport for the first time or after a lay-off, or for those with a history of injury or who have suffered a disability or condition which has hindered or prevented them taking regular exercise.

It is important also for those who have or have recently had a heart condition or high blood pressure, asthma or other respiratory problems, arthritis or joint trouble, especially in the back or legs.

Above all, if *you* have any doubt about the effect of regular strenuous exercise on your health, seek medical advice.

Fitness Testing

With a clean bill of medical health, or if you do not feel that a medical check-up is necessary, the next stage is to discover how fit you are.

The fitness tests described on the following pages were devised many years ago and are used as a way of finding out *progressive* levels of fitness. The essence of these tests is that if you cannot perform them without undue effort – this means without breathlessness (and the truest measure of that is whether or not you can carry out a normal conversation) you should not proceed to the next test.

For most people these tests are a formality. The tests themselves are simple, painless and speedy. For the young and healthy they hardly arouse so much as a gentle sweat; but for others – and this series of books is aimed at a broad spectrum of ages and fitness levels – some of the tests may cause severe breathlessness and discomfort. If at any time you do feel discomfort *stop*, and consult medical opinion. And, if you cannot proceed beyond a certain test, it means that your stamina is wanting and you should undertake a conditioning programme.

Fitness Tests

The fitness tests listed below are in four stages of increasing difficulty. In addition, a parallel test for pulse rate is shown which specifies more exactly the relative state of your fitness. For anyone regularly engaged in sport these tests are very basic indeed, but for those who are beginning or who have been inactive for some time, they will provide a useful assessment. It is important that you should be completely healthy when carrying out these tests. If you have a cold, cough or other ailment, wait until it has subsided.

Fitness Test 1: Stairs

Walk up and down a flight of 10-15 stairs three times. (*If at any time during this exercise you feel at all uncomfortable – stop.*) At the end you should be hardly breathless and be able to carry on a normal conversation without puffing. If this is the case, proceed to fitness test 2.

Fitness Test 2: Jogging on the Spot

Making sure that you lift your feet a good 20 cm (8 in.) off the floor, run on the spot/jog on the spot for *three minutes*. (*If at any time during this exercise you feel at all uncomfortable – stop.*) Once again at the end you should be able to carry on a normal conversation. If this is the case, proceed to fitness test 3.

Fitness Test 3: Step-ups

Take a strong chair (the *second* step of the stairs used in the first test will do) – the important thing is that the rise should be not less than 35 cm (14 in.) – and step up and down (right leg up, then left leg to join it so you are standing on the chair, then left leg down, followed by right leg down, etc.). Do this briskly for *three minutes* (*two minutes* if aged over 45). (*If at any time during this exercise you feel at all uncomfortable – stop.*) You should be able to carry on a normal conversation after this test. If so, proceed to fitness test 4.

Fitness Test 4: Measured Run

Mark out a measured 1.6 km (1 mile) and then gently jog the distance. (*If at any time during this test you feel at all uncomfortable – stop.*) At the end you should be mildly breathless and your times should be as follows:

Under 45	*Men*: 10 minutes
	Women: 12 minutes
Over 45	add one minute for each span of five years

If you are slower than these times you will need to undertake further stamina-improving exercises. Otherwise, when you can perform this test without discomfort or distress, you should be fit enough to start gaining fitness for your chosen sport.

Pulse Rate Test

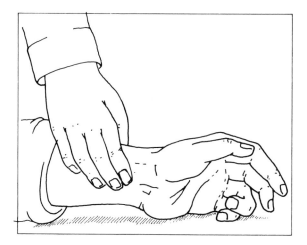

To take the pulse, first place your watch, with an easily seen second hand, where you can observe it. Then, using a pile of large books, a step or stout box – about 20 cm (8 in.) high – step up and down briskly for *three minutes*. (*If at any time you feel at all uncomfortable – stop.*) Rest for *one minute* and take your pulse for one minute. To do this, place three fingers of the right hand on the left wrist some 3 cm (1 ½ in.) below the mound of the thumb (*see illustration*). You should then be able to feel your pulse and count the beats. Check your rating with the table below. (The lower the pulse rate, generally the fitter you are.)

	Men	*Women*
Excellent	below 68	below 76
Good	68-79	76-85
Average	80-89	86-94
Below average	90-99	95-109
Very poor	100+	110+

If your score is *average* or better, you should be fit enough to start gaining fitness for your chosen sport. If it is *below average* or worse, you should undertake some further stamina-building programme.

The Elements of Fitness

There are three main elements of fitness:

suppleness
strength
stamina

and all three need to be worked on to attain general fitness. In addition, in some sports *muscle endurance, speed* and *agility* can also be important. Where applicable, exercises for these will be found in Section II.

Suppleness

(also called flexibility, or mobility)

Suppleness is the degree of movement in the joints and muscles of the body (this includes the neck, back and limbs). A gradual stiffening of the joints is a characteristic of the ageing process, and also occurs through disuse. When this happens, people are far more susceptible to strains and sprains. General suppleness is more important for some sports than others, but specific suppleness is needed in most sports, and suppleness exercises are designed to help develop the maximum range of the joints, limber up the whole body, and reduce the risk of injury.

Strength

Strength broadly means muscle power. And strength can be improved in two ways, through *isometrics* or *dynamics* (also known as isotonics).

Isometrics

Isometrics are essentially static exercises against resistance, and are intended specifically for building up muscle bulk. As such they are much used in body building, or in restoring wasted muscle after injury. They involve little or no movement and, as a result, cannot be used as stamina-improving exercises. Further, they could be dangerous for those over 35 or with high blood pressure.

Dynamics

Dynamics are exercises which do involve movement. In these, the resistance gives way and this has the effect of stretching the muscles. In addition, repetitive exercises have a strengthening effect – through alternately shortening and lengthening the muscles – and, if continued for a sufficient length of time, can also improve stamina (*see below*). Dynamics are in greater general use and have far greater application in sports fitness. Most dynamic exercises take the form of rhythmic activity, e.g. jogging, swimming, skipping.

Stamina

(also called heart and lung endurance or, sometimes, aerobics)

Stamina is essentially staying power – the ability to keep going without undue breathlessness. The muscles of the body are kept fuelled with oxygen carried in the blood stream (their waste products are also borne away in the blood stream). During strenuous exercise the muscles use oxygen at a very rapid rate, if this is not replaced quickly enough the muscles cease to function, and this is the essence of fatigue. Furthermore, the inefficient removal of waste products adds to muscle fatigue and painful exhaustion takes over. In sport, a tired person obviously cannot perform to the best of his or her ability and is also susceptible to injury. Stamina-building exercises aim to increase the efficiency of the heart and the muscles, and improve the circulation of the blood, thus rendering fatigue less likely.

Balanced Fitness

The aim of these exercises is to achieve a *balanced fitness* – extra suppleness keeping pace with improved stamina; strength married with greater flexibility – in short a programme which pays attention to all three components of fitness and exercises all the important parts of the body properly. Circuit training is the most popular way of combining these exercises, and this is discussed in more detail at the end of this section.

How you choose to regulate your exercise is up to you, for training is a matter of personal discretion and individual preference, provided that certain guidelines are adhered to and the regime is gradual and progressive.

Exercise Sessions

It is usually considered that it is necessary to carry out three sessions a week to maintain reasonable standards of fitness. Each session should last about 30 minutes in the following proportion:

20 minutes warm-up and stamina building
10 minutes split between suppleness (*two to three minutes*) and strength (*seven to eight minutes*).

Exercises should be enjoyable. If you lose motivation, *stop*, for the odds are that you will not be doing the exercises correctly to get maximum benefit from them and, if you allow your concentration to lapse, you could injure yourself.

Never exercise to the point of distress or complete breathlessness, on the other hand don't be afraid to break into a sweat. The golden rules of exercise are:
exercise conscientiously;
never to the point of distress;
never to the point of complete breathlessness;
exercise regularly;
exercise gradually, but progressively.

Suppleness Exercises

When doing these exercises it is important to stretch gradually. Push until it feels slightly uncomfortable. Hold for a second or two, then relax and repeat. For rolling exercises, rotate the part on as wide an arc as possible so that you feel you have moved over the full range.

In general, suppleness exercise sessions work systematically through all parts of the body – neck, shoulders, arms, chest, trunk, hips and legs. Repeat movements five to ten times with progressively more effort.

Spine and Hips

1 *Side Bends*

(Standing erect, with feet comfortably apart, hands at sides.)

Bend trunk to the left and at same time slide

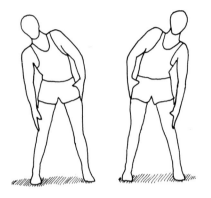

hands down the calf as far as possible keeping the back straight. Return to the upright position. Then repeat on the other side.
Starting repetitions: 6 each side

2 *Trunks Twists*

(Standing erect, with feet comfortably apart, hands on hips.)

Twist the trunk alternately from side to side, keeping the back as straight as possible.
Starting repetitions: 6 each side

Spine, Hips and Hamstrings

3 *Alternate Toe Touches*

(Standing erect, with feet comfortably apart, arms raised.)

Bend down and touch the opposite toe – e.g. right hand to left toe. Then return to the upright

Drop chin to the chest and then slowly roll the head round reaching as far over the shoulders as is comfortable. Repeat clockwise and anti-clockwise.

Starting repetitions: 10

Shoulders

5 *Shoulder Shrugs*

(Standing erect, with feet comfortably apart, hands hanging loosely at the sides.)

Raise shoulders as high as you can shrug and then pull them down as far as you can.

Starting repetitions: 15

6 *Wing Stretchers*

(Standing erect, with feet comfortably apart, arms parallel with ground and folded as in the drawing.)

position and touch the right toe with the left hand, and so on. It is important to return to the upright position with the back straight.

If you cannot touch the toes, reach down as far as is comfortable. As you become more supple you will find that you can reach down further and further.

Variation: carry out the exercise sitting down.

Starting repetitions: 6 each side

4 *Neck Rolls*

(Standing, or sitting erect [this is an exercise which can be done at any time] with feet comfortably apart, hands on hips.)

Force the elbows back as far as they will comfortably go. Count two, and relax. The body should remain upright and the head erect.

Starting repetitions: 10

13

Arms and Upper Body

7 *Arm Circles*

(Standing erect, with feet comfortably apart, arms forward at shoulder height as in the drawing.)

Bring the arms upwards brushing the ears, then around to the starting position. Flex the wrists and fingers while doing so.

Variation: hold the arms out sideways and describe small circling movements which

gradually get larger until the full swing is achieved.
Practise both forwards and backwards.
Starting repetitions: 6

8 *Arm Flings*

(Standing, erect, with feet comfortably apart, arms held as in exercise 6, but with fingertips touching.)

Fling first the left arm out as far as it will comfortably go (keep it parallel to the ground, there is a tendency to let it droop.) Then return to the central position and repeat with the right arm. Keep the body and head erect throughout the exercise.
Starting repetitions: 10

Wrists

9 *Wrist Shakes*

(Standing [or sitting] erect.)

Hold out arms. Let the hands droop and then shake the wrists and hands up, down and sideways, keeping the forearm still throughout.
Starting repetitions: 15 seconds

Abdomen, Thighs and Calves

10 *The Reach*

(Standing erect, with feet comfortably apart, hands hanging loosely at the sides.)

Breathe in deeply and slowly bend backwards, at same time reach upwards with fingers outstretched. Breathe out. Hold position for 5

seconds before returning to the upright position. Breathe in deeply, then repeat.

Starting repetitions: 6

11 *The Lunge*

(Standing erect, with feet comfortably apart, and hands on hips.)

Stride sideways with the right leg pivoting the feet as in the drawing. Adopt a lunging position as in fencing. Keep pushing the right leg back, and keeping it straight at the same time, while forcing the body towards the floor. Hold for a count of 5, relax and repeat with the other leg. Keep the back straight throughout and the forward leg vertical.

Starting repetitions: 4 each side

12 *Hurdles*

(Sitting on the floor, as in the drawing, with right leg outstretched and left leg bent at right angles.)

Place hands on top of right leg and reach down towards the foot, bending the body, neck and head as close to the leg as possible (at first it will

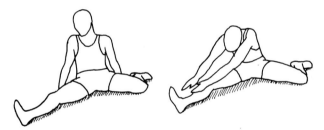

not be possible to reach very far down the extended leg, but as suppleness increases this will improve). Do not overstretch or bounce. Apply a steady pressure only, then relax. Repeat on other side.

Starting repetitions: 5 each leg

15

Upper Legs

13 *Leg Swings*

(Standing erect, with feet comfortably apart, arms outstretched. For balance hold on to a chair, table or door handle.)

Swing the outer leg backwards and forwards as far as you can comfortably go. Relax and repeat on the other side.

Starting repetitions: 6 each side

14 *Knee Pulls*

(Lying flat on the ground.)
Pull first one knee, then the other – or both knees – into the chest. Hold for a count of 5, then relax and repeat. Either keep the head on the floor or bring it forward to the knee.

Variation: stand erect and lift one knee as high as you can and clasp it to the chest. Hold for a count of 5, then relax and repeat with the other leg.

Starting repetitions: 4 each leg

Lower Legs

15 *Calf Stretches*

(Standing at arm's length away from a wall, with the feet together and hands together.)
Lean forward, bending the arms and keeping the feet flat on the floor. Straighten and relax. Repeat.

Variation: this exercise can also be used to strengthen the fingers by pushing the body upright using the fingers rather than the hands.

Starting repetitions: 15

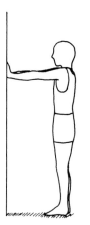

Strength Exercises

These exercises are designed primarily to strengthen muscles and ligaments and, by the use of high repetition, to improve muscle endurance.

Strength exercises work on the 'overload' principle, where repetitions or resistance, or both, are gradually increased.

It is a great mistake to launch oneself into strength exercises without adequate warm-up (see p.27), otherwise there is a high risk of pulled muscles, etc.

The exercises below are graded by degree of difficulty

* easy
** difficult
*** very difficult

Do not attempt the most difficult until you think you can manage them comfortably.

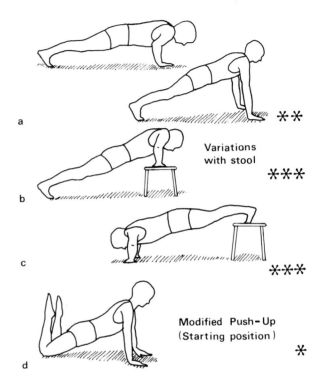

Body, Arms and Shoulders

1 Push-ups (Press-ups)

Degree of difficulty:
Normal**
With stool***
Modified*

(Lying on the floor face downwards, feet together and hands under the shoulders.)

Push the body off the floor by straightening the arms. Then lower the body to the floor by bending the arms. It is important to keep the back straight.

Variations: try using a stool, as shown in illustrations (b) and (c), for greater strenuousness (see star gradings).

The modified push-up is an easier variation (see drawing [d]).

Starting repetitions: 6

Arms and Shoulders

2 *Pull-ups*

Degree of difficulty:
Normal* * *
Modified* *

(After finding a strong bar just out of reach of the upstretched arms.)

Jump up and grasp it, either with palms facing the face or away from it, as shown. Hang for a moment, then slowly pull the body up until the chin is level with the hands. Hold, then relax and repeat. Try to avoid swaying, and keep the feet together.

a

***

The modified pull-up is based on the position of suppleness exercise 15, but with the feet further from the wall, as shown in illustration (b). Push the body upright until the arms are straight, then bend the arms and allow the body to fall forward

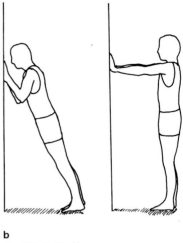

b
Modified ✳ ✳

again. Using the fingers helps strengthen them. Make sure your footing is secure.
Starting repetitions: 4

3 *Hip Raises*

Degree of difficulty: *

(Sitting on the floor, with legs and feet together and hands placed flat on the ground.)

Raise the body using only the hands, until the arms are straight. Hold for a count of 5, then relax and repeat. The body should be vertical and arms completely straight when raised from the floor.

Variation: by placing a book/books under the hands the exercise can be made more difficult.
Starting repetitions: 8

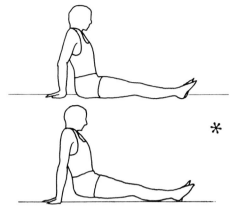

Wrists and Arms

4 Broomstick Roll

Degree of difficulty: *

(Standing erect, with feet comfortably apart.)
Take a length of broomstick about 1 in. in diameter and 2 ft long, having tied a length of string to the centre point long enough to be 3-4 in.

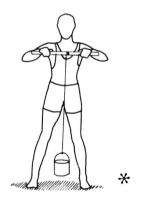

from the floor. To this is tied a weight – plastic bag of sand, a brick, a tin can holding water, etc. (start

with a light weight and build up). Then, using both hands, palms down, wind the string on to the broomstick.

It is easier to do the exercise with the elbows bent and hands close to the chest, as in the drawing. Then carry out the exercise with the arms straight in front.

When the weight reaches the top, slowly wind it down again.

Starting repetitions: 6

5 Tennis Ball Squeeze

Degree of difficulty: *

Taking a tennis ball, two squash balls, or other rubber ball, in the hand, squeeze as hard as you can. Hold for a count of 5 seconds, relax and repeat.

Variation: hold the tennis ball in front of you, with arms straight and fingers of both hands interlocking. Squeeze the ball as hard as you can until you feel the effect in the shoulder muscles. Hold for 5 seconds, then relax and repeat.

Starting repetitions: 6

6 Fingertip Push-ups

Degree of difficulty: ***

This is an adaptation of the push-up (strength exercise 1) using the fingers rather than the flat of the hands (see illustration).

Starting repetitions: 4

***

7 Fingertip Hip Raise

Degree of difficulty: **

This is an adaptation of the hip raise (strength exercise 3) using the fingers rather than the flat of the hand.
Starting repetitions: 6

**

Abdomen

8 Bicycling

Degree of difficulty: **

(Lying on the back as shown in the illustration.)
Carry out a bicycling movement with the legs. Pull back the knee as far towards the face as comfortable then straighten it fully.
Starting repetitions: 10 seconds

**

9 Bent-leg Sit-ups

Degree of difficulty:
*Normal***
*Variation****

(Lying on the back, legs bent and arms to the side with the feet under a low bar – wardrobe, chair or sofa – or with someone holding the ankles.)
Raise the body *slowly* to a sitting position leaning forward, trying to touch the knees with the head. Then *slowly* return to the sitting position.

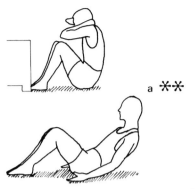

a **

b Variation ***

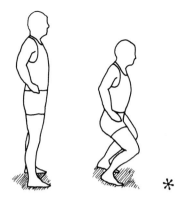

*

Variation: try a trunk twist at the top of the sit-up. Later, exercise without a foot support, as in illustration (b).

It is wrong to use the hands as a lever to assist or hold the position. Place the hands behind the head to remove temptation.

Starting repetitions: 4

Thighs and Legs

10 *Half Squats*

Degree of difficulty: *

(Standing erect, with feet comfortably apart, hands on hips.)

Rise on the toes and *slowly* sink down, bending the knees until the half-squat position is adopted. Hold for count of 5 seconds, then stand upright again. Relax and repeat.

Keep the body upright, the tendency is to lean forward.

Starting repetitions: 6

11 *Squat Thrusts (Burpees)*

Degree of difficulty: **

(Start as shown in illustration)

Shoot out the legs behind you into the push-up position, and then bring them forward again. Keep the feet together at all times.

Starting repetitions: 6

**

12 Sprinters

Degree of difficulty: **

A variation on squat thrusts (burpees), but using only one leg at a time. Keep the back straight at all times.
Starting repetitions: 6

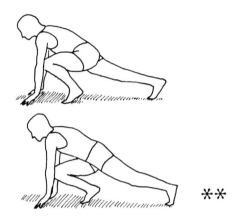

**

13 Paint Can Raises

Degree of difficulty: *

(Sitting on a chair or bench, with thighs parallel to the ground and lower legs at right angles.)
Take a paint can, or similar object which can be filled to the extent required to give weight, and hook it on the toe of one foot. Raise the weight *slowly* until the leg is straight, and then *slowly* lower it to the ground again. Repeat, and then change legs.
It is important to keep the knees together. Grasping the chair will make the exercise easier to start with.
Starting repetitions: 6

*

14 Leg Raises

Degree of difficulty:
Single *
Double **
Side *

(Lying flat on the back, with hands on the floor, palms down.)
Raise one leg *slowly* about 9 in. then *slowly* lower it again. Relax. Repeat with the other leg.

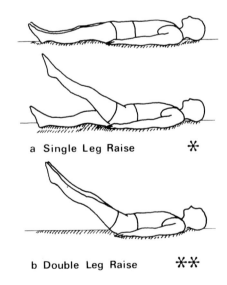

a Single Leg Raise   *

b Double Leg Raise   **

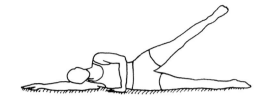

c Side Leg Raise　　　　*

Variations: double leg raises and side leg raises, as illustrated in (b) and (c).

It is important to keep completely flat on the floor, including the head. Using the hands to help lever the legs will make the exercise easier to start with, but should be resisted as soon as possible.

Starting repetitions: 6

15 *Step-ups*

Degree of difficulty: **

(Standing erect, with hands at the sides facing the chair, stool or pile of large books 12-18 in. high.)

Place the right foot on the stool and, by using only the power of the legs, raise the body until standing on the stool. Step down again *slowly.* Repeat with the left leg. The body should remain upright throughout. There is a tendency to lurch forwards when mounting the stool. At first put the whole foot on the stool, later use only the toes.

Starting repetitions: 6

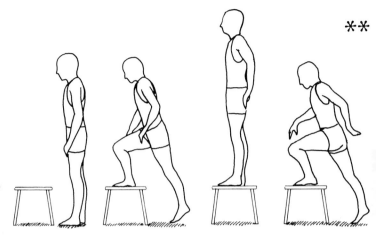

**

16 *Bench Jumps*

Degree of difficulty: **

(Standing alongside a bench, pile of books or bricks.)

Jump with feet together from one side to the other, and back again.

Variations: jump with feet astride, landing on the bench; hop on one leg either onto or over the bench; carry a weight, jumping on the toes rather than the whole foot, etc.

It is important to stand upright, there is a tendency to lurch either forwards or sideways. Carried out at speed, bench jumps are an excellent stamina-building exercise.

Starting repetitions: 6

Lower Legs

17 Shin Strengtheners

Degree of difficulty: *

This is a variation on paint can raises (strength exercise 13). Instead of raising the whole leg,

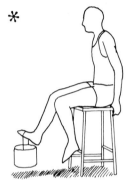

raise only the foot, bending at the heel. It is important to raise and lower slowly. Hold at the high level for a count of 5 seconds, then lower. Repeat, then change the can to the other foot. Holding on to the bench or chair while doing the exercise is a help to start with, but should be resisted later.
   Starting repetitions: 4

18 Calf Raises

Degree of difficulty: *

(Standing erect with arms at the sides, toes on the edge of a shallow step, or large book.)
   Bring the arms forward and at the same time rise on the toes. Lower *slowly*, relax and repeat.

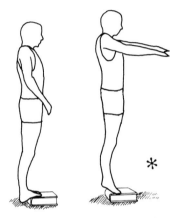

The body should remain upright throughout; there is a tendency to lean forward.
   Variation: instead of rising fully on the toes, rise only halfway, and hold the position for a count of 4-5 seconds.
   Starting repetitions: 6

Stamina-building Exercises

As applies for all exercises, those for stamina building should be regular – 20-minute sessions, three times a week is ideal.

Walking

Walking is probably the best way gradually to build up stamina for the unfit, the partially fit, or those who have not been taking regular exercise for some time.

This should not be just a gentle amble, but a purposeful exercise; breathing in deeply and keeping the back straight and the head up, walk briskly, lengthening the stride and the distance gradually.

Jogging

Jogging is probably the most popular form of stamina building. It is also an excellent exercise at the start of a warm-up routine (see p.28).

Running/Jogging on the Spot

This is a excellent exercise provided the legs are lifted high enough (30 cm [12 in.]). It is also useful for strengthening the leg muscles, particularly the hamstrings.

Skipping (rope work), bicycling and swimming are all good stamina-building exercises as are certain strength exercises if performed sufficiently vigorously at high repetition. These include:

Push-ups, modified if necessary (Str. 1)
Pull-ups, modified if necessary (Str. 2)
'Bicycling' (Str. 8)
Squat thrusts (Burpees) (Str. 11)
Step-ups (Str. 15)
Bench Jumps (Str. 16)

Build up your repetitions gradually, but make your routine progressive.

Circuit Training

Circuit training is nothing more than a range of exercises (eight to ten is usual) concentrating on different parts of the body. The mix comprises suppleness and strength exercises, so stamina building must be additional to the basic circuit, unless the circuit is done at sufficient intensity to constitute a stamina-building routine in itself. There are a number of criteria in choosing and using a training circuit:

1 The circuit should start with warm-up exercises to tone up the muscles and prevent muscle strain.
2 No two successive exercises should work on the same part of the body, thus giving variety.
3 The training programme must be progressive and comprehensive.

Within these parameters the choice is wide and

entirely personal. Three examples of circuits to help attain general fitness are listed below.

Method

First of all go through the whole circuit to familiarise yourself with the exercises – this is particularly important for the not-so-young and the not-so-fit – making sure that each exercise is carried out properly.

Having absorbed the general requirements of the circuit, you can get down to circuit training proper. Remember, never force yourself, and you should never be more than moderately breathless.

It is useful and interesting to keep a check on progress, so have a clock or watch handy. Start off by doing each circuit three times at your own speed, and then pausing for five minutes before doing another series. Time each series. The point of keeping times is to enable you to judge when you have reached a plateau in your training and the time has come for a variation. Such variation should be *gradual* and *progressive*.

The asset of circuit training is that it is possible to alter the routine in many different ways:

1 By doing the circuit faster.
2 By increasing the number of circuits before pausing.
3 By decreasing the pause time between circuits.
4 By increasing the number of repetitions within the circuit (and if you feel that you need to work on any particular weakness you can adjust accordingly); it is usual to start on a low number of repetitions and work up.

5 By adjusting the circuit at any time if it starts to become monotonous and you want a change. A further bonus is that by keeping the 'exercise content' constant within the circuit, it is possible to develop stamina by decreasing exercise time gradually.

Sample Circuits
(*starting repetitions in italics*)

Always begin with a preliminary warm-up: jog/run on spot for one minute; rest one minute; jog/run one minute.

Circuit A

Neck rolls (*Sup. 4*) (*10*)
Step-ups (*Str. 15*) (*6*)
Arm flings (*Sup. 8*) (*10*)
Calf raises (*Str. 18*) (*6*)
Bent-leg sit-ups (*Str. 9*) (*4*)
Squat thrusts (*Str. 11*) (*6*)
Shoulder shrugs (*Sup. 5*) (*15*)
Trunk twists (*Sup. 2*) (*6 each side*)
Half squats (*Str. 10*) (*6*)

Circuit B

Shoulder shrugs (*Sup. 5*) (*15*)
Bent-leg sit-ups (*Str. 9*) (*4*)
Knee pulls (*Sup. 14*) (*4 each side*)
Squat thrusts (*Str. 11*) (*6*)
Hip raises (*Str. 3*) (*8*)
Leg swings (*Sup. 13*) (*6 each leg*)
Push-ups, (modified if necessary) (*Str. 1*) (*6*)
Alternate toe-touches (*Sup. 3*) (*6 each side*)
The lunge (*Sup. 11*) (*4 each side*)

Circuit C

Side bends (*Sup. 1*) (*6 each side*)
Push-ups, (modified if necessary) (*Str. 1*) (*6*)
Leg swings (*Sup. 13*) (*6 each leg*)
Squat thrusts (*Str. 11*) (*6*)
Arm flings (*Sup. 8*) (*10*)
Bent-leg sit-ups (*Str. 9*) (*4*)
Shoulder shrugs (*Sup. 5*) (*15*)
Step-ups (*Str. 15*) (*6*)
The lunge (*Sup. 11*) (*4 each side*)

These circuits can be done at home, in the open or in a gymnasium and, if there are facilities available, make use of them (consult the resident instructor on how to incorporate them into your training circuit). But with a bit of ingenuity certain other exercises can also be done at home using everyday or easily obtainable items.

Warming-up and Warming-down

Warming-up

The purpose of warming-up, which is perhaps the single most important element in sports fitness, is twofold:

1 To tune the participant both mentally and physically.
2 To lessen the chance of injuring unprepared muscles.

With time at a premium and sports facilities expensive and in high demand, the tendency for most players is to rush into their sport at maximum power and speed. Nothing could be more calculated to lead to injury. It is essential to warm up beforehand, both physically and mentally and this pays dividends far in excess of the time expended on it. A number of players, especially if accustomed to a warmer climate, take a hot shower before play (a hot bath is too enervating) and raise the body temperature to the most favourable point for intense muscular activity. Warming the muscles relaxes them and improves muscle response; it also has the effect of stretching the muscles and making them less prone to injury if violently used. Mental warm-up is important to ease stress and tension before a match or game and generally to key the mind to the forthcoming test.

Warming-up, for the most part, consists of some jogging (running/jogging on the spot when the former is impracticable) and some simple stretching exercises – particularly of those parts of the body which are most used. Warming-up should be taken to the point of sweating, except in those sports where a lot of waiting is involved.

Method

Carry out six to ten repetitions of general stretching exercises as described on pages 11 to 16. Particularly valuable are:

Arm flings (*Sup. 8*)
Toe touches (*Sup. 3*)
Side bends (*Sup. 1*)
Trunk twists (*Sup. 2*)
The lunge (*Sup. 11*)
Arm circling (*Sup. 7*)
Calf stretch (*Sup. 15*)
Knee pulls (*Sup. 14*)
Wrist shakes (*Sup. 9*)
Neck rolls (*Sup. 4*)

Further details of warming-up exercises are given in Section II.

Warming-down

Warming-down is almost as important in the prevention of incapacitation as warming-up. Cold, damp clothes next to the skin are a prime source of chills and, for the more elderly, could lead to

muscular aches. Particularly susceptible are those parts of the body where clothing has been restricted – the waist, crotch, feet, armpits and back. It is sensible after play to put on a sweater to keep the muscles warm, and to walk about after exercise carrying out a few suppleness exercises to prevent the muscles stiffening up.

The purpose of the warming-down process is to allow the body to cool down gradually. It is also sensible and hygienic to take a shower or bath as soon as you can, and to take the opportunity to massage stiff or sore muscles while they are under water. This applies particularly to the neck and shoulders. If a hot bath or shower is impracticable, a brisk rub with a towel will also help prevent irritating after-sport stiffness.

Weight and Fitness

The weight factor is as significant an element in fitness for sport as it is in general fitness. In sport, if you are overweight you are likely to be short of stamina and will tire sooner than your opponent, but in addition you will also be placing yourself at greater risk through injury. It has been shown conclusively that the more tired a sportsman or sportswoman becomes, the more prone he or she is to injury. For when fatigue strikes concentration lapses, the natural reflexes are blunted, and muscles seem no longer to be mastered by the brain.

In additon, if overweight, you expose yourself to such problems as shortness of breath, varicose veins, backache, arthritis, chest troubles, high blood pressure and diabetes (both these last two can lead to heart conditions), and other ailments and disabilities.

The table below shows a suggested weight to height ratio.

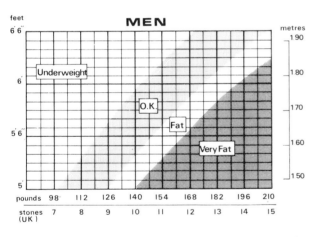

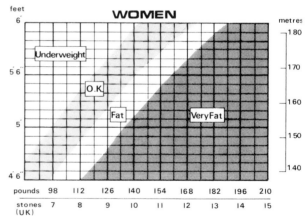

Diagram courtesy Health Education Council

SECTION 2
Fit for Rugby

Introduction

Rugby is a game of skill and courage where physical contact is a basic ingredient and physical fitness an essential element in the preparation of the player. The fundamental and unique appeal of the game is that, because of the variety of skills required in different positions, it is possible for individuals of all shapes and sizes and abilities to participate. Ranging indeed from the diminutive nine-stone scrum-half, like Jacques Fouroux, the famous French scrum-half and coach, to the giant six-and-a-half foot, 17-stone second row forward, such as Maurice Colclough of England and the British Lions. Each can play their part successfully in what is one of the most enthralling of team sports.

Not so many years ago it was possible to reach a high level in the game provided you had what could be called 'natural ability' and, if you were a forward, a certain amount of physical presence. Today, however, standards in most sports, rugby included, are so high that only players who are prepared to work hard at their game, both on and off the field, have any real chance of success.

If you have any sort of aspiration you must be constantly learning, practising and refining techniques and skills. You must be sure that you are in peak physical condition and capable of dealing with the tremendous demands of a sport in which you can be smashed to the ground, involved in a prolonged wrestle for the ball and be expected to sprint 60-70 yards (60-70 metres), all in the space of a few minutes. You must also ensure that you are in the right condition to deal with the particular physical demands of your position – those of a prop forward differ considerably from those of a wing three-quarter.

The unfit player is a liability to his team, both in the game and in training sessions, because he is unable to perform the individual and team skills of which he knows he is capable and because he is persistently in a state of fatigue or even exhaustion. The purpose of this book is to explain the fitness requirements for the inexperienced but up-and-coming and ambitious young (or otherwise) player, and then to provided a plan of campaign, which will ensure that he has few fitness problems. This will also guarantee that he will derive much more enjoyment and satisfaction from his own performance.

There is no short cut to fitness in rugby. Fitness training has to be a continuous, progressive process, because there is no limit to how fit you

Ireland's superb goal-kicker, Ollie Campbell, showing great suppleness required for efficient kicking action (*photograph* © *Bob Thomas*)

33

Ireland's scrum-half, Robbie McGrath; suppleness and agility in passing action (*photograph* © *Bob Thomas*)

can become, and must be geared to your own requirement, position, physical conformation, etc. It is hard, but rewarding, and can be enjoyable work, particularly if you happen to be a masochist! The rewards can easily be seen in a well-planned training programme because you soon find you are capable of both longer and more intensive bouts of exercise. You find that you have a greater resistance to fatigue, you recover more quickly, you can handle the intense skill practices without difficulty, and you are more likely to avoid serious injury. You enjoy your game more because you find you are faster and more agile in avoiding and

making tackles, you are stronger for making tackles really count and winning the ball, you can last longer during sustained periods of play and, finally, you are still going well at the end of 80 minutes.

Self-help Philosophy

The emphasis and philosophy in this book is one of self-help. The player who relies totally on his coach and the one, or at most two, training sessions per week for all his preparation is unlikely to achieve the standards of which he is capable. He must be prepared to work on his fitness at home and use the club sessions for skill practice and team work. Any fitness training done in a club session should be an additional bonus, and the player who prepares in his own time will find that he can approach these sessions in a much more relaxed frame of mind, and can concentrate totally on his skill work because he knows that he can cope adequately with the physical demands upon him. Naturally, his skill development will increase that much more quickly and make him a much better player.

You might think from what has been said so far that you are expected to train for 24 hours a day but, in fact, one and a half to two hours a week is sufficient to produce significant fitness effect, and details of how this can be achieved will be explained later.

Fitness Training Sessions

A few years ago, if one went along to a club training session, the fitness programme would most likely consist of a steady jog round a field and some arm swinging to loosen up, several frantic lung-bursting sprints, and perhaps a set of muscle-tearing exercises like press-ups and sit-ups. Although there is still a suspicion of this around, there is now a general emphasis on careful planning of the fitness sessions so that they reflect the actual needs of the game and the individual player.

Legendary Welsh fly-half, Phil Bennett, showing agility and elusiveness in beating two All Blacks (*photograph © Bob Thomas*)

The Fitness Needs of Rugby

If we have a look at the game in terms of physical demands we can get some idea of the sort of fitness which is required in rugby. Rugby is a game of start and stop, with bouts of intense activity separated by short rest periods thankfully provided by the referee's whistle. In fact, in a typical 80-minute game of Rugby Union, there are approximately 150 pieces of action which last for a total of 25-30 minutes. Some movements last for only a few seconds, e.g. scrum-half passes to fly-half who kicks into touch, and no more than 15 per cent of the movements last for more than 20 seconds. Long, sustained periods of play are few and far between and if they occur in big matches they produce some of the greatest rugby spectacles, such as Gareth Edwards' try in the famous All Blacks v. Barbarians match, or Phil Bennett's try under the posts in the last few minutes for Wales against Scotland at Murrayfield. Most of the running action is in short, sharp bursts, nearly always between three-quarter and full pace, and it has been worked out that a typical player would cover an average of 4000-5000 metres during the course of a game. In between the running, the player is involved in a number of bouts of physical contact and the extent of these will vary according to his position. For example, there are likely to be about 40 scrums, which will last about 20 seconds each, in which all forwards are involved, and some players will be involved in 20 or more bone-crunching tackles. In these situations strength is of paramount importance.

Armed with this sort of information, it is now possible to construct fitness training programmes which are more related to the particular requirements of rugby and, even more important, to particular positions.

Welsh centre, David Richards; exceptional balance and agility while demonstrating passing action on the run (*photograph* © *Bob Thomas*)

Elements of the Fitness Programme

First Get the Principles Right

Whatever the sport, the planning of a training programme has to be based on sound principles, and in fitness training the principles are related to the effects that certain types of exercise have upon the body. The principles are the same for all sports, the programmes and the methods will be different for each sport and this chapter is concerned with an explanation of these principles with particular emphasis on rugby.

What we are trying to do in fitness training is to improve the exercise efficiency of the body in such a way that it enables the player to deal with the physical demands of the game. We are trying to create improvements in the working of the heart, general body circulation and of the muscles and joints. By causing improvements in the functioning of these body parts and systems there will naturally be improvements in the components or elements of fitness.

These may be classed as follows, and in rugby terms:

1 *Suppleness:* the ability to move the body parts through a wide range of postions, e.g. hooker positioning and striking for the ball in the scrum.

2 *Strength:* ability to exert great force, e.g. centre performing bone-crunching tackle.

3 *Stamina:* continuous, strenuous general body activity e.g. flanker continually on the move.

4 *Local Muscle Endurance:* ability to use individual muscle groups for sustained periods of time, e.g. mauling or wrestling for the ball.

5 *Speed:* ability to run at a great pace, e.g. winger sprinting for the line.

6 *Agility:* ability to adjust position and change direction at speed, e.g. side-stepping fly-half.

Each player according to his position will need to develop each of these components to a greater or lesser extent and his fitness training methods will be prepared accordingly.

Overload

Now we have progressively to build up the fitness of the player so that he can more than meet the demands of the game. This involves the principle of *overload*. This simply means that the body must be pushed beyond its normal limits so that it is under some considerable pressure. This is where commitment and dedication is called for, and it does require hard work and it does hurt. The rewards are in the improvement of performance because the body adapts to the increased levels of exercise and can then be pushed to further limits – and the improvements are plain for all to see! The aim in training should be to overload the system so that ultimately we reach a stage where the body never becomes overloaded in the game – an ideal which is rarely achieved. Sebastian Coe recently said that with the intensity of modern training the race should be a rest day!

Training should always be harder than the game – e.g. if you do not cover 4000-5000 metres in a training session of 80 minutes you will never survive it in a game.

Training Progression

There must be a continuous and steady *progression* in fitness training – you must always aim for new peaks because, as previously stated, there are no limits to fitness. So the principles of progression must be adhered to. Continue to overload systematically and never be satisfied with your performance. This will enable you to work harder and more effectively during the game and produce better and better performances.

Reversibility

Now we come to the soul-destroying aspect of any form of practice and training: if it stops, we start to slide back. This is the principle of reversibility. So you must avoid breaks in training at all costs – dedication is now critical and, if there are unavoidable breaks due to injury, you must try to work even harder to get back to your original level. It is not all bad though because you do retain some element of fitness for a considerable time and at least you do now know your capabilities. This makes it that much easier to get back to your original level again. Obviously, even the most dedicated trainers have to have a break from time to time, and once you become experienced you are able to deal more easily with the natural peaks and troughs of performance.

Specificity

It is desirable at first to try to develop an all-round general fitness level using a training programme in which all fitness elements are considered, and this is the purpose of Section I of this book which deals in general terms with sports fitness requirements and describes a range of exercises to that end. This creates a sound base from which to specialise. However, the role of the prop forward and the full-back are quite different both in techniques and skills and in fitness requirements. So it is necessary for each player to concentrate on the particular components of fitness which are needed for his position. For example, the prop would need to improve his upper body strength and muscle endurance while the full-back is more likely to need work on his speed and agility. Therefore, the principle of specificity dictates the tailoring of each individual's training programme.

So, overload, progression, reversibility, specificity – never forget them! Always use them!

Measurement

Once the training programme is under way there should be a steady improvement in fitness and this will soon start to show, both in increased training levels and improved playing standards. It is very important that the player can recognise these improvements easily because, in the week-by-week routine of training, it is quite easy to forget what you were like when you started. A sound idea, therefore, is to make sure you record your starting points and then set yourself a series

England's Paul Dodge showing balance and speed in breaking between Ray Gravell and Clive Rees of Wales (*photograph* © *Coloursport*)

of targets or goals which can be reached as a result of your training.

Keep a careful check on your progress and you will soon begin to realise the considerable improvement made in your fitness. This can easily be done by compiling a training diary which will contain brief details of your training schedules and sessions on a day-to-day or week-by-week basis. From time to time it is valuable to give oneself little tests (*see p.67*), designed to illustrate ability and development in a particular fitness component and, by making a note of results, progress can be measured. We are now

bringing a little science into our training and this can only be good!

Warming-up and Warming-down

No intensive fitness work should commence until you have prepared your body thoroughly for action. This requires a gradual build-up of activity so the body, particularly the muscles and joints, is eased into the position where it is ready for the instant high-powered action which is part and parcel of rugby training and playing. The values of the 'warm-up' have already been discussed in Section I but it is particularly important for rugby because of the physical nature of the game.

Warm-up

About 10-15 minutes should be devoted to the warm-up and it should allow a simple basic plan:

1 Easy jogging for a minute or two to shake up the muscles generally and get the circulation going.
2 General stretching, flexing and mobility exercises of the muscles and joints to be used during the game or training (*see pp.11-16*).
3 More strenuous activities like striding, squat jumps, high knee raising and astride jumps.
4 Movements which are related specifically to the skills to be used in training or game with a gradual build-up to near maximum effort.
5 Finish the warm-up feeling nice and loose, perspiring gently, only mildly fatigued and ready for action within one or two minutes.

Warm-down

Finally, if you have had a really strenuous work-out and if you finish temporarily exhausted, try not to collapse in a heap and then stagger off to get changed and showered. It is very useful to wind down with some gentle jogging and loosening exercises just to bring the muscles and body slowly back to normal, then have a nice long bath or shower. This wards off the possibility of stiffness and soreness which is otherwise likely to occur.

Try to make sure you follow all the above practices and you will not go far wrong.

Planning the Programme

It is easy to operate like a robot and be programmed by the coach so that you religiously perform the tasks he set during the training sessions. This has its importance, but is only part of the preparation for a dedicated player. Much of the spade-work is done by the individual and he should spend some considerable time working out a carefully planned, season-long programme for himself. Take as much advice as possible, ask your coach and other experts for help and use this book.

First of all it is necessary to look at the factors which will influence the planning of your programme in order to ensure that what you intend to do is both realistic and within your capabilities. You will need to ask yourself a number of fundamental questions:

How much time have I available?

Demonstration of power and agility by two giant lock forwards in line-out in England v. Ireland match (*photograph © Coloursport*)

Where am I going to do my training?
What training will I do at the club during squad sessions?
What and when are my playing commitments?

It is no good getting carried away with ambitious, and over-exuberant plans which become so time-consuming that they are impossible to maintain. All sorts of things will interfere even with the best-laid plans – such as extra problems at work or at home, or with wife or girlfriend, social engagements etc. Bear in mind that you may have to modify your plans at no notice at all, so work out on that basis how much time you can realistically afford, and then plan accordingly. It is so much better if you can occasionally put in an extra training session rather than be forced to miss one out.

You will normally be committed to at least one club training session and one match per week. To supplement sessions at the club it seems reasonable to suggest that one and a half to two hours more per week on fitness training is well within the compass of players keen to do well.

Fitness training does not take all that long, provided it is specialised and intensive. It is possible then to work out a programme involving two 45-60 minute sessions, or, alternatively, three 30-40 minute ones. A typical week during the season might look like this:

Saturday: match
Sunday: rest
Monday: first fitness session (45-60 minutes)
Tuesday: club training or second fitness session (45-60 minutes)
Wednesday: rest
Thursday: club training or second fitness session (45-60 minutes)
Friday: rest

If fitness sessions are shorter than the prescribed 45-60 minutes, train on Wednesday as well. If the season has not yet started try to add a session over the weekend, and perhaps another to take the place of club training.

England and Ireland forwards in mauling confrontation where strength and muscle endurance are essential (*photograph* © *ASP*)

In order to produce improvements in any component of fitness it is necessary to work on each component at least two to three times per week. Generally the greatest improvement in fitness should occur during pre-season training, while during the season fitness should be maintained at a constant level with perhaps a little extra effort before a really big match.

Before getting down to planning any detailed schedule you should first of all check on the facilities available in the immediate vicinity – only the most dedicated will be prepared to travel miles for a short fitness session, and it is no good planning an elaborate weight-training routine if there are no weight-training facilities for miles around! Basically all you need is a place to run and exercise – even the street and backyard or garage will do. However, in these days there is almost always a local park, running track, sports field or leisure centre within easy reach. Decide which of the facilities you need, check on their availability and then plan your training programme accordingly.

In the first place you will need to plan a general programme designed to produce improvements in all components of fitness and this should then be adapted according to your particular needs, and the type of training already covered in club sessions. If you have a fitness fanatic for a coach who flogs you half to death all evening with energy-sapping stamina runs and exercises (a typical approach), then you should concentrate in your own work on quality training involving speed, agility and strength. On the other hand, your coach may be one of the new school who believes that club training is all about skills and tactics, in which case, although there will be some incidental fitness work, you will need to plan a much more comprehensive fitness programme involving all fitness components. Once you are under way you will begin to recognise more precisely what your personal requirements are. You will then be able to adjust your programme to suit the needs of your particular position or design to counteract any general weaknesses which may appear.

Last, and most important, your programme must be worked out in relation to your playing season and to your match to match commitments. Basically it should follow three distinct but overlapping phases: pre-season, during season and post-season training.

Post-season Training

If one bears in mind that the season lasts for eight months (September – April) or even longer, it doesn't seem as though there is much of a pre- or post-season and the temptation might be to collapse after the last match and eat, drink and be merry while avoiding all forms of physical exercise until the start of the next season. This possibly sounds highly attractive and is no doubt a philosophy followed by many, but it would be a serious mistake to switch off completely. By all means relax and enjoy yourself at the end of the season, but, for the first two months, you should keep your fitness hand in by playing another sport (tennis, golf, etc.) or do some regular running, swimming or cycling. Nowadays training for the half-marathon is all the rage – you could do worse!

Pre-season Training

This is probably the most critical, and you should begin a gradual build-up as the season approaches so as to reach a peak in time for the first match. There is nothing worse than going on to the field for the first match knowing that you are unlikely to last the pace – you have no excuse. You have had four months to get ready!

Pre-season training should commence in earnest about *eight weeks* before the first match, devoting *four weeks* to general stamina work (*see p.24-26*), gradually introducing more quality work over the last period when club training probably gets going. Once the season has begun you should develop a fairly strict weekly routine which the most dedicated among you will stick to come hell or high water!

If you intend to reach your maximum potential in rugby, training has to become an all-year ritual and it is essential to plan your training programme accordingly. Get your diary out now and make a start, and then well before the beginning of each season, settle down and try to construct a scheme which will take you through the whole year. It will pay handsome dividends.

Exercise Routines

As already mentioned the principal components of fitness in rugby are:

Suppleness
Strength
Stamina
Local Muscle Endurance
Speed
Agility

For the rugby player each of these components must be developed systematically and trained quite independently of each other. So let us look at each one to see how they can be attained.

Suppleness

Work on suppleness provides a basis for all fitness training. It should never be neglected and consists of a series of stretching and flexing or mobility exercises of the major muscles and joints, so that the player is able to move the essential parts of the body over the maximum possible range. A full range of suppleness exercises are given in Section I (*pp. 11-16*).

You should develop a regular five to ten-minute routine at the beginning of every training session and before every match as part of your warm-up. It is beneficial in itself and also ensures that the body is in a suitable condition to undertake the more strenuous action to follow.

If you have had a really exhausting session or match the previous day and do not really feel up to another heavy outing, it is very beneficial to have a session concentrating solely on mobility work with gentle stretching and flexing and perhaps a little easy running. This should take about 20 minutes and you will soon feel like a new man.

Any suppleness routine should follow a number of simple guidelines:

1 Perform both stretching and flexing exercises.
2 Move the body smoothly and rhythmically and

avoid jerking, bouncing or quick movements. Try to relax the parts of the body you are not using.

3 Move the part of the body which you are intending to exercise to a position where it feels slightly uncomfortable and continue to exert pressure for a second or two. Then relax.

4 For rolling movements (as with the shoulders) rotate the part in as wide an arc as possible so that you feel that you have moved over the full range.

5 Repeat each movement five to ten times with progressively more effort.

6 Work systematically through all parts of the body – neck, shoulders, arms, chest, trunk, hips and legs.

7 Perform more specific exercises which apply to your particular position, e.g. hooker – hip and shoulder mobility; scrum half – shoulder rotation, groin stretchers to help receiving and passing from line-out and scrum.

Strength and Muscle Endurance

Strength and muscle-endurance training is one of the essential elements in the schedule of any top-class forward. Scrummaging techniques are now very advanced and rucking, mauling and tackling require so much sheer strength that forwards who neglect this aspect of their training will find it difficult to survive at anything above a superficial level. For backs, it is different. Strength training certainly has its value, but as a back you need to be very selective about the nature and type of training you do, and this will depend on the type of player you are and also your particular position.

Strength depends largely on the size of the muscles, so basically the bigger you are the stronger you are and there is no doubt that the giant 'gorilla-like' prop forward could eat for breakfast the diminutive opposition scrum-half – if he could catch him! However, with the correct training it is possible to make tremendous increases in the size of your muscles and therefore bring about significant improvements in strength – just look at the body builders for example.

You can only build muscle bulk onto your basic framework, so obviously there is a limit to the level you can reach. Nevertheless, it is important that you try to establish the strength requirements for your particular position and work effectively to achieve them. One very important asset of strength training of major relevance to backs, is that it can lead to improvements in speed and power (see p. 62) and it is essential to include strength training in your programme if you need to develop these aspects of your game.

Of all the components of fitness, strength and muscle endurance are the most open to improvement. Further, these improvements are the most easily identified. Absolute strength – how much weight one can physically lift – is naturally the quality of the big man, but what is almost as valuable in rugby is the ability to handle your own body weight. This is where the smaller man has a distinct advantage because he can improve his relative strength to a much greater degree.

As has been mentioned, if you are unable to keep up your training, either because of injury or some other reason, muscles tend to waste away or atrophy very rapidly. One of the great virtues of strength training is that specific weaknesses can be rectified quite quickly. On the negative side, neglect of this type of training can lead to a rapid fall off in strength and this can be the cause of serious injury, especially to muscles or joints. The points about regular and progressive training have been emphasised before, but it has particular relevance in strength training because, although rapid improvements can occur, the reverse applies almost as quickly if you stop – so keep up the good work!

There is a close relationship between strength and local muscle endurance because both concern the working capacity of the muscles. But whereas strength involves the ability to perform a single act with maximum force, muscle endurance involves the ability to sustain the use of the muscle for a period of time. The use and value of local muscle endurance in the game of rugby is confined mainly to scrummaging and mauling. This is of critical importance to all forwards, but the back who can maul and wrestle like a forward is often a great asset to his side.

Strength and muscle endurance can be improved by using weight-training methods, and this creates two possible problems if you wish to incorporate this work into your fitness-training programme. Firstly, access to weight-training facilities where individual weights and multi-gym units are available is obviously essential. These may usually be found, if not in your own club, at least at your local sport or leisure centre, or even at the relatively new and emerging health and fitness clubs. Secondly, weight-training, particularly for strength, can be very dangerous if you are not well acquainted with the required techniques. The risk of injury is great when moving heavy weights and it is essential that you are given some expert advice and tuition before attempting any form of weight-training.

Weight-lifting and training is a sport in itself and we cannot attempt in this book to provide all the details, but just to make a start you should take note of the following points:

1 Select a series of exercises (six to eight) which enables you to work on different groups of muscles – legs, trunk, shoulders, arms, etc.
2 For each exercise, work out the weight (resistance) to use so that you can do no more than 10 repetitions (for strength) and between 10 and 20 (for muscle endurance).
3 The number of repetitions you can do in one go is referred to as a set and you should eventually try to complete three sets in a training session.
4 Each muscle group should be rested after each set. During this time other muscle groups can be exercised so that most muscles may be trained in one session on the lines of the circuit method of training.
5 When you reach a maximum, i.e. ten repetitions for strength on a particular exercise, increase the weights.
6 Try to do at least three sessions per week initially (pre-season) for most rapid improvement and then keep going with one or two sessions per week (during season).
Note: Take it easy on your first few sessions (perhaps using fairly light weights) until you get used to the techniques and to avoid too much stiffness – and make sure you take good advice.
7 Make the exercises as closely related as possible to the needs of your position. If necessary take advice and discuss with your coach.

Using the body as a means of resistance is of great value in muscle-endurance training – such exercises as chins (pull-ups), dips, press-ups, trunk curls (bent-leg sit-ups), squat jumps and squat thrusts, particularly when it is not possible to use proper weight-training equipment. If you can obtain a set of mini-weights – simple dumb bells and a number of discs and a bar – it is possible to arrange a programme using a combination of body resistance and weights which can quite easily be done at home.

The following illustrations show a list of useful exercises (*see also Section I, pp.17-24*) from which you can choose six to eight to make up your programme:

Legs

Half squat (Str. 10 and illus.)
Calf raises (Str. 18 and illus.)
Hamstring pulls (illus.)
Leg presses, single leg; both legs (illus.)
Step-ups, with weights (Str. 15 and illus.)
Squat jumps (illus.)

Trunk

Trunk curls, without weights (on inclined bench) (illus.); with weights behind head.
Leg lifts on inclined bench (illus.) – assists thighs as well.
Back arches, with weights behind head, legs only supported (illus.) Back lifts (illus.)

Upper body (Arms, Shoulders, Chest)

Arm curls (illus.)
High pull-ups (Str. 2 and illus.)
Shoulder press, front of head; behind head (illus.)

Bench press, pulls to behind neck; pulls to chest (illus.)
Wrist rolling, using bar, rope and weights (wind up the rope on the bar with weight hanging from rope) (Str. 4)

Once you become proficient in the exercises and schedules it is quite easy to adjust your programme to create different demands by adding or subtracting weights, speeding up or slowing down repetitions, working more explosively, or having shorter or longer rest periods. All these variations help to make the programme more interesting, but one thing is certain and that is that you must be prepared to work your muscles until they feel like lead on each exercise and stick closely to the principles of training to produce a worthwhile effect.

Half squat using multi-gym – start   Finish

Half-squat using bar-bell – start

Finish

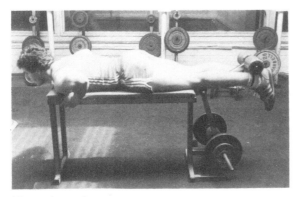

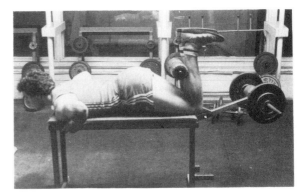

Hamstring pulls – start

Finish

Leg presses using multi-gym – start

Finish

Leg presses using leg press machine – start

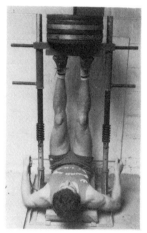

Finish

Step-ups with weights – start

Step-up to full standing position on bench

Squat jumps with
weights – start

Jump up as high as
possible

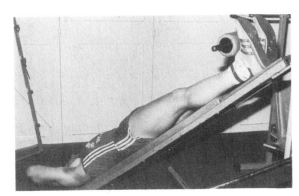
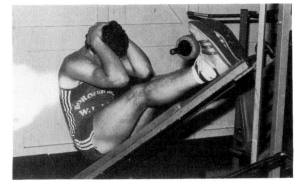

Trunk curls on inclined bench – start

Raise elbows to knees

Leg lifts on inclined bench – start

Raise legs above head

Back arches – face down, weight behind head,
feet supported

Back lifts – start,
standing upright, bar-bell
resting on shoulders

Lower as shown

Arm curls using multi-gym – mid position (start arms full extension)

Final position

Arm curls using bar-bell – mid position (start with weight resting on thighs)

Final position

High pull-ups – start – hang from chin bar arms fully extended

Raise chin to bar

Shoulder press using bar-bell – start with weights resting on shoulders/chest

Finish

Shoulder press using
multi-gym – start

Finish

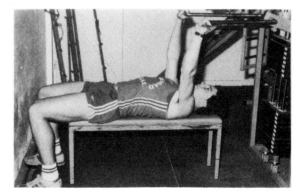

Bench press using multi-gym – start

Finish

Bench press using bar-bell – start

Finish

Arm pulls using multi-gym – start

To behind neck

To chest

Stamina

Now we come to the crunch. How well does your body stand up to the great physical demands of a strenuous 80-minute game – could you play 30 minutes extra time in a vitally important cup match? Everything we have dealt with so far in this chapter has been concerned with quite specialised areas of fitness designed to develop quite specific components, but now we need to look at the more general aspects of fitness involving the ability of the whole body to sustain as high a work rate as possible for as long as possible.

The ideal in rugby is to keep going with maximum effort throughout every incident in the game and then still be able to produce something more at the end, although it is doubtful if any player could do this in every match. As we have already said, rugby is a game of fits and starts, and no two games are the same. In some games, either by use of particular tactics, or by over-zealous refereeing, there are more stops than continuous play, while in others the game will flow from end to end in waves of non-stop action for most of the 80 minutes.

In rugby it is very difficult to pace your game because at one moment you may be called upon to sustain your effort for one or even two minutes, and then do it again almost immediately. Then again you may find for long periods that you are only working for a few seconds at a time. It is quite easy to run yourself ragged in the early part of the game and then be unable to contribute sufficiently later, and it is also quite easy to drift through a game without really extending yourself by not getting involved more than is absolutely necessary. Obviously, both these approaches

would be wrong and the inexperienced player is likely to encounter these difficulties but, if he knows that he has trained hard, and is confident that his stamina is good, he will be able to contribute more and the desire will be there.

The stamina demands vary from position to position, with the greatest pressure probably being on the back row and scrum-half. Jean-Pierre Rives, for example, is an illustration of almost perpetual motion – pushing in the scrum one second, winning the ball on the ground or in the maul the next, and then trying to get in support of a passing movement or covering frantically to tackle the opposing three-quarters. Wingers and centres, on the other hand, tend to make their own work and may have long periods when they are comparitively inactive before they are suddenly called upon to take part in two or three long, passing movements, one after the other, when they are running with the ball, supporting other players and getting back quickly into position again. All the forwards need stamina in plenty so that they can get to breakdown after breakdown, first there as often as possible, and be there in numbers to make sure of winning the ball. Whatever the situation, the more stamina you have the more ready and capable you will be of dealing with whatever arises.

For training purposes there are two types of stamina you need to work on. First of all, it is important, particularly for front- and second-rows, and possibly for the half-backs, that they can 'trundle' around the field almost continuously, at a fairly even pace, without undue exhaustion, and then be able to put in a big effort when required, perhaps in a ruck or maul or on a quick break. Secondly, it is important, particularly for back-row forwards and to a lesser extent centres, wings and full-backs, that they are putting everything in for as long as possible before exhaustion sets in and performance falls away. This cannot be sustained for much longer than a minute, after which it is essential to recover within seconds ready for the next effort.

There are a number of guidelines for stamina training:

1 There are two distinct types of training: steady state work and exhaustive work.
2 In steady state work you should maintain as high a work rate as possible without needing a rest period.
3 In exhaustive work you have to be prepared to put in maximum effort for as long as possible and then repeat the exercise with only a short recovery period.
4 Always work to precise times, distances and/or repetitions so that progress and improvement can be measured.
5 If you plan to do quality work on speed and agility or strength in the same session always do this before the stamina work.

Best results can be obtained by using the following training methods:

Continuous Runs

Running at a steady pace (over a set distance — minimum two miles, maximum five miles), or run for a fixed time (minimum 10 minutes, maximum 40 minutes), and measure the time taken or distance covered.

This is good, but hard, for front and second rows and, to a lesser extent, back rows and half-backs.

Fartlek Runs

Again covering a set distance or running for a fixed time, but on this occasion varying the pace between fast striding, easy running, jogging and walking.

Good for back rows and half-backs, and useful for all other players.

Interval Runs

A running track, rugby pitch or other suitably marked area is necessary here.

This type of training involves performing several separate runs for set distances or set times at above steady state pace with a short rest or recovery period between each run. Running distance should normally be between 100 and 600 metres, at times between 15 and 120 seconds.

Rest Periods: the length of the rest periods between each run depends on the speed of recovery. A rough guide is when breathing has become fairly steady again, but usually not more than two minutes.

Target times and distances should be set in relation to initial performances and the improvements should be measured as training progresses: e.g. three 600 metre runs with two minutes' rest between each, with a target time of two minutes per run. If this time is adhered to then the target should be lowered.

There is an infinite variety of schedules for interval running but you should work on the general principle of a 20-30 minute session (including rests), and you should increase the

number of repetitions, change the target times and distances and cut down the length of rest periods as your fitness improves.
The following are a few examples:

1 10 x 100 metre runs; 30 second rest; initial target: 15 seconds per run.
2 6 x 200 metre runs; 1 minute rest; initial target: 35 seconds per run.
3 4 x 400 metre runs; 1½ minute rest; initial target: 80 seconds per run.
4 3 x 600 metre runs; 2 minute rest; initial target: 2 minutes per run.
5 Pyramid runs; 100 to 200 to 400 to 600 to 400 to 200 to 100 metres; 1 minute rest between runs; initial target for complete pyramid: 13 minutes (including rests).

Any combination of these schedules can be used to make your 20-30 minute session. This type of training is probably the most popular and most beneficial to all players.

Shuttle Runs

This is another popular form of training and again is beneficial to all players because it combines exhaustive work with agility.
Shuttle runs are an important ingredient in speed and agility training (*see p. 62*) and these may be adapted for stamina training by increasing the number or distance of the shuttles so that you can maintain full pace throughout the runs. Runs should then be repeated after a short rest period. Distances between turns may vary from 10-40 metres.
This is a very similar type of training to the interval runs but brings in the element of agility and has the particular advantage that it can be performed in a fairly confined area. Here are a few examples:
1 8 x 10 metre shuttle; eight runs with 30 seconds' rest between runs; initial target: 25 seconds.
2 6 x 20 metre shuttle; six runs with 1 minute rest between runs; initial target: 35 seconds.
3 4 x 40 metre shuttle; four runs with 1½ minute rest between runs; initial target: 45 seconds.

Circuits
(*see also Section I, p.25*)

This type of training is an all-purpose method which should lead to improvements in strength, muscle endurance and stamina. It involves a series of 'different' exercises completed as quickly as possible one after the other with a set number of repetitions in each exercise.
Outlined below are two circuits which you will find are quite simple and require no complicated equipment, but nevertheless are very demanding if performed properly.

Exercises	Repetitions (according to level)		
	A	**B**	**C**
Bend and stretch (Sup. 9 and illus.)	10	15	20
Squat thrusts (Str. 11 and illus.)	15	20	25
Sit-ups (Str. 9 and illus.)	9	12	15
Squat jumps (illus.)	10	15	20
Back arches (p. 51)	10	15	20
Burpees (as for squat thrusts, but beginning and ending in standing position) (Str. 11 and illus.)	10	15	20
Star jumps (illus.)	20	30	40
Press-ups (Str. 1 and illus.)	10	15	20

Bend and stretch – start

Finish

Squat thrusts (burpees); start in press-up position, shoot knees up between the arms

Throw legs back to press-up position as quickly as possible

Sit-ups – start

Finish

Squat jumps – start in crouch position and jump as high as possible fully stretching the body . . .

. . . return to crouch position in one movement

Star jumps – from standing position feet together, jump into the air, splitting legs apart but keeping them fairly straight; land with feet together again; use small bounce between each jump if necessary

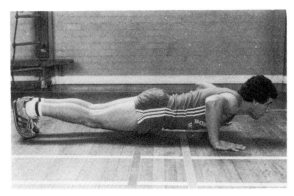

Press-ups

Exercises	Repetitions		
	A	**B**	**C**
Bend and stretch (Sup. 9 and illus.)	10	15	20
Shuttle runs (illus.)	4	5	6
Sit-ups (Str. 9 and illus.)	9	12	15
Shuttle runs (illus.)	4	5	6
Back arches (p. 51)	10	15	20
Burpees (11 and illus.)	10	15	20
Shuttle runs (illus.)	4	5	6
Press-ups (Str. 1 and illus.)	10	15	20

Procedure:

a Choose level A, B or C (start at A if uncertain and work up).

b Complete repetitions for exercises one to eight as quickly as possible and maintaining good technique.

c Return to exercise one and follow through the circuit again, and then a third time.

d Record time taken and try to improve time in each session.

e When you can continue through three circuits with little or no rest periods either move up a level or increase the number of repetitions in the exercises which you find the easiest.

Shuttle run – start

Sprint

Turn

Sprint back

Speed and Agility

There is no substitute for speed in rugby. If opposing players get there before you, the loose ball is lost, the support is cut off, the tackle is missed and the try is made. No matter whether you are a Gerald Davies or a Billy Beaumont, and whatever your position or size, you should always strive to improve your speed as much as possible.

Rugby is also a game of stop and start and quick change of direction, whether you are on or off the ball. In avoiding the tackle (Phil Bennett's sidesteps), getting up quickly after a tackle, diving on a loose ball, changing direction when play is switched, the agile player will always have an advantage, so work on agility should go hand in hand with speed training.

Nobody is going to turn a 16-stone prop forward into a flying winger – some people's bodies are made for sprinting and others are not – but everyone can make themselves quicker. Speed depends on how well the muscles work (particularly the legs), on how fast they will work, how far they will stretch and how strong they are.

Once you get beyond the basic fitness level there is not much you can do about making the muscles work faster, but you can make them stretch further (*see Suppleness, p. 11*) and you can definitely make them stronger and therefore more powerful.

Training to improve speed and agility requires very intense activity for short periods of time. Quality of performance is of major importance and every exercise should be performed at maximum or near maximum effort. Take special note of the following points:

1 Because you are putting the muscles under severe strain make sure you have completed a good warm-up to avoid muscle strains.
2 Continue with each exercise only until the first sign of fatigue. If you are struggling for breath, or your muscles start to ache, stop immediately, for you will start to lose quality, and this is no good for developing speed and agility.
3 Try to maintain good technique and rhythm in all exercises while working at 90-100 per cent effort. *Do not strain*, keep a smile on your face!

4 Let your body (breathing and muscles) recover before you start another bout of exercise.

5 Always do speed and agility training *before* stamina training, and not after.

6 20-25 minutes is usually sufficient for a really good session on speed and agility. Do it two to three times a week and you will soon be like lightning.

Here are a number of exercises which you will find useful:

For Improving Leg Strength and Power

****1** Squat jumps (p. 50)
****2** Tuck jumps (illus.)
****3** Star jumps (p. 60)
 4 Squat thrusts (burpees) (Str. 11 and p. 59)
****5** Bench jumps
    or
    Bar jumps (Str. 16 and illus.)
 6 Bunny hops (illus.)
 7 Alternate knee lifts (illus.)
 8 On the spot sprinting

*To make these exercises more demanding, it is possible to carry weights such as dumb bells or medicine balls.

Tuck jumps – from standing position, jump into the air, tucking knees up as near to the chest as possible; use small bounce between each jump if necessary

Bench jumps or bar jumps – stand astride a low bench (about 12 inches high) or at the side of a bar or rope . . .

Bunny hops — as for squat jumps, except jump forward as far as possible each time

. . . jump continuously on and off the bench or over the bar or rope

Alternate knee lifts

Running Exercises

1 Stretches: from standing start, build up pace running easily and relaxed to 60-70 per cent maximum over 40-50 metres, slow down gradually over 20-30 metres.

2 High knee runs: from standing start, using bouncy steps and high knee action. Complete 25-30 steps over about 30 metres.

3 Fast leg runs: from standing start, using short bouncy steps, moving legs as fast as possible. Complete 40-50 steps over about 30 metres.

4 Wind sprints: from rolling start, accelerate to 90-100 per cent sprinting pace and continue for 30 metres.

5 Bounding: long bounding strides, concentrating on maximum bounce over 40-50 metres. Do not over-stretch.

6 Shuttle runs: (4 x 10 metres or 4 x 15 metres) Short sprints between two lines a set distance apart. Quick turn after placing foot on limit line. Keep low and accelerate out of turn.

7 As for shuttle runs, but start from back lying position – feet on starting line.

8 As for shuttle runs, but start from front lying position – hands on starting line.

9 As for shuttle runs, but start on hands and knees.

10 Sidestepping runs: run from side to side down narrow channel (5 metres width) as fast as possible stepping on marking lines with outside foot over 40 metres (6-10 sidesteps).

11 Swerving runs: as for sidestepping runs, but step on marking lines with inside foot, swinging free leg across in swerving action.

Whenever you do a speed and agility session choose a selection of the above exercises and runs to make up your 20-25 minute schedules. You can experiment with them all in the first place and then decide which you are going to do in each session. Each exercise has its own particular value so you should vary your selection as much as possible so that they are all incorporated into your training at the same time.

Using longer distances, more repetitions and shorter rest periods these exercises can be adapted for stamina and endurance training (*see* p. 55).

Preparing Schedules

You should now be ready to put together your training schedules and, providing you adhere closely to the principles, methods and exercises presented in the previous pages, it is possible to build up your own programme with schedules which suit your own personal needs.

This particular section will give you some ideas by presenting a basic plan which can be adjusted to fit in with your particular requirements and problems.

First of all you should divide the training into three major categories:

Pre-season
During season
Post-season

Now decide how much time you will have available at each stage and approximately which days and how many days in each week you will be able to train.

The following is an indication of the type of programme you should expect to follow.

Pre-season

Length of period: eight weeks
Weeks 1-4: general fitness (5-6 hours per week)
Weeks 5-8: fitness and skill work; club training

In weeks 1-4 with probably no club training and no matches you should be able to train on 3-4 days including weekends. In weeks 5-8, weekends will still be free and should provide the opportunity for extra fitness work.

The time spent on each training session should be fixed to suit you, but generally should last between 40 and 90 minutes depending on the time you have available and what sort of training you intend to do.

The following time blocks are recommended and could apply to both pre-season and during-season periods.

90-minute Blocks

		Minutes
a	Flexibility (warm-up)	10
	Speed and agility	20
	Strength and muscle endurance	30
	Stamina (steady run)	20-30
b	Flexibility	15-20
	Speed and agility	20-30
	Stamina (exhaustive work)	30-40

45-minute Blocks

a	Flexibility (warm-up)	15
	Speed and agility	30
b	Flexibility	10
	Strength and/or muscle endurance	35
c	Flexibility (warm-up)	10
	Stamina (exhaustive work)	15-20
	(steady work)	15-20

60-minute Blocks

a	Flexibility (warm-up)	10
	Speed and agility	20
	Stamina (exhaustive) or strength	30

Fit the blocks into each week's training schedule so that you achieve a target total of five to six hours each week in weeks 1-4, and in weeks 5-8 adjust the schedules to fit in with club training demands.

In weeks 1-4 concentrate on stamina work and start your weight training if you think you need it. Introduce quality work or speed and agility and specific strength work after week 2.

In weeks 5-8 try to keep the schedules going alongside club training, particularly by making good use of the weekends.

The pre-season training period is the most crucial because it is the time when the greatest improvements in fitness can be made in order to reach peak condition for the first match.

During Season

The basic aim of the fitness work during the season is to try to maintain the standards you reached in the pre-season training, and, as previously mentioned, this can be done by supplementing the club training with an extra two hours of fitness work per week – if you can fit in more than that, so much the better.

Probably the most important elements are speed, agility and strength. Stamina work is complemented by club training and matches, but do not neglect it, particularly if you've missed a match or had only club sessions or matches.

Use the same schedules as in your pre-season sessions and try to fit in at least two quality sessions on speed and agility and/or strength per week. This is the minimum requirement to maintain your pre-season standards. Front-row and second-row forwards should concentrate on strength work with some steady running and either strength or speed and agility. Three-quarters should concentrate on speed and agility.

When the really big matches are coming up, try to fit in one or two extra sessions to ensure that you are up to the extra physical and mental demands which will be necessary.

Post-season

This should be a fairly relaxing period, but as previously stated, don't switch off completely. Most rugby players take part in other sports anyway, but in case you do not, try to make sure that you continue with some form of exercise during the 'rest' period. You will find life so much more difficult if you don't. Regular jogging, cycling or swimming is very useful, but if this does not appeal, more formal competitive activities, such as tennis, squash and athletics, are just as valuable.

Whatever schedules you decide on, get your training diary out and make a thorough plan for the season and then record your progress. You will find this very helpful in ensuring that you are keeping to the right principles and providing excellent motivation to keep at it.

Checking Progress

Setting yourself targets is a great motivating factor in fitness training and, by recording your day-to-day progress in a training log or diary, you can keep a close check on your improvements. For example, in the running schedule outlined in the previous section, initial targets have been presented and progress can easily be checked by comparing performances after four or eight weeks' training. If you are really training hard, it will be surprising and rewarding to see how much progress you have made. If you are conscientious about recording your performances you will know that you are getting fitter.

To help you even more, there are a number of fairly simple tests which you can do from time to time throughout the season. These are designed to measure particular elements of fitness. By comparing the results of these tests from the beginning to the end of the season, you can see exactly how well or how badly you are doing. Testing once a month is probably the most advantageous.

The Tests

Touch-turn (Suppleness)

Stand, feet at shoulder-width apart, back to wall, feet 6 inches (15 cm) from wall. Keeping hands together, touch ground between feet and turn to left to touch wall at shoulder level directly behind you. Touch ground again and then twist to the right and touch wall. Repeat, counting maximum repetitions in one minute.

Score minimum 40 repetitions; maximum 60 repetitions.

Shuttle-run – 5 x 20 Metres (Speed and Agility)

Sprint backwards and forwards between two lines 20 metres apart. Touch line with foot at each turn. Best performed in a gym or sports hall or on a hard surface outdoors.

Score minimum: forwards 24 seconds; backs 18 seconds.

Vertical Jump (Explosive Power/Speed)

Stand sideways against a wall and raise inside arm to reach as high as possible. Place a mark on the wall. From standing position, and without bouncing, jump up and reach as high as possible to touch the wall above the mark. Measure distance reached above first mark. Make three attempts.

Score minimum: forwards 16 inches (40 cm); backs 18 inches (45 cm); maximum: forwards 28 inches (70 cm); backs 30 inches (75 cm).

Press-ups (Strength/Muscle Endurance)

Front support position, body straight, hands underneath shoulders. Lower to ground touching with chin, chest and hips simultaneously. Push up to front support position again. Complete maximum number or stop after one minute – no rests.

Score minimum: forwards 20; backs 25; maximum: forwards 60; backs 70.

600-metre Run (Speed/Stamina)

On running track, rugby pitch or other suitably marked area, run as fast as possible over a distance of 600 metres.

Score minimum: forwards 130 seconds; backs 120 seconds; maximum: forwards 95 seconds; backs 85 seconds.

12-minute Run (Stamina)

On running track, rugby pitch or other suitably marked area, run as fast as possible for 12 minutes. Measure the distance covered.

Score minimum: forwards 2800 metres; backs 3000 metres; maximum: forwards 3800 metres; backs 4000 metres.

Conclusion

In conclusion, let me just emphasise the great value of fitness in the game of rugby. Without ever under-estimating the importance of technique and skill, the All Blacks, the Springboks, and, more recently, the 1982 Australian Rugby League tourists, have shown that the results of matches can depend on which is the fitter side. The Australians indeed have been universally recognised as one of the fittest teams ever seen and their results have proved the point – undefeated and the most successful touring side ever.

Everyone has the opportunity to be superlatively fit. The guidelines have been provided in this book. So go to it . . . and good luck!

SECTION 3
Ailments and Injuries

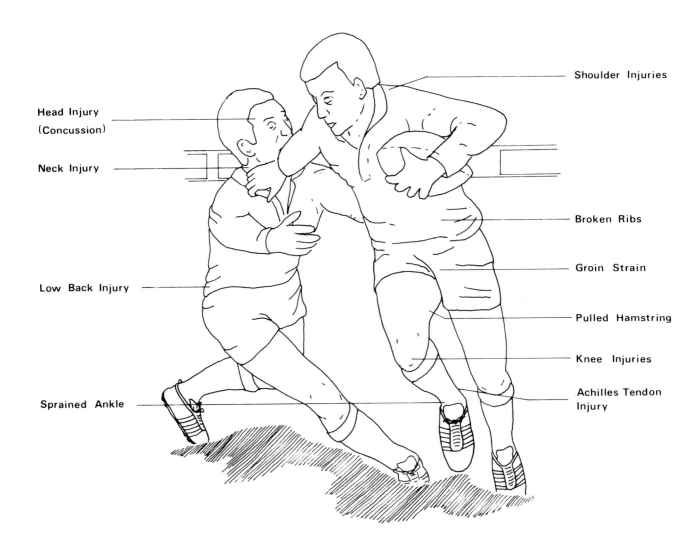

Head Injury
(Concussion)

Neck Injury

Low Back Injury

Sprained Ankle

Shoulder Injuries

Broken Ribs

Groin Strain

Pulled Hamstring

Knee Injuries

Achilles Tendon
Injury

Rugby injuries

Introduction

Any physical exertion can cause a variety of aches and pains and this is as true with sport as with any other exercise. Each sport has its own spectrum of typical ailments and injuries, for the most part caused by sudden trauma or repeated wear and tear. Some can be prevented by having a good degree of prior fitness and training, but sportswomen and sportsmen are well advised to know something of the specific injuries that they could sustain when playing their chosen sport.

Specific Injuries Associated with Rugby

The illustration indicates the range of injuries to which rugby players are particularly susceptible. But it should be emphasised that many players — often through maintaining a high level of fitness, and attaining it before the season begins — may play through season after season without injury.

However, in a contact game of the nature of rugby, accidents and injuries can happen and the medical advice in this section could prove of considerable importance in reducing the effect of injury and enabling a player to get back into the game more quickly. It is useful for every player, as well as referee or linesman or coach, to recognise the symptoms of the more serious injuries.

As would be expected with such a hard-hitting contact sport, most of the typical rugby injuries are due to direct or indirect impact rather than over-use. Cuts, grazes, bruises, sprains, strains, dislocations and fractures are commonplace. Every part of the body has a blacklist of likely injuries.

Head and Face

Usually *cuts, bruises* or *fractures* resulting from kicks or treads. Often a more specific injury, such as a black eye, broken nose, cut lip, or torn ear occurs in the scrum, ruck, line-out or tackles. These are dealt with under General Ailments and Conditions on p. 78. A particular problem with open wounds is the risk of *tetanus* from contamination by mud. Superficial cuts and grazes are less at risk, but deep cuts and penetrating wounds could harbour tetanus and it is important to seek the protection of an anti-tetanus injection.

Head injuries resulting in *concussion* are all too frequent in rugby. Boot-to-head and head-to-head contact can knock a player out and may risk more permanent brain damage. For emergency treatment of head injury, see First Aid on p. 86. For any head injury involving temporary loss of consciousness, the player should not try to continue the game.

Neck

The most likely injuries are caused by the whiplash effect of indirect impact to the trunk during a heavy tackle or wrenching of the neck during a neckhold. Pulled neck muscles, strained ligaments or even a fracture-dislocation (broken neck) can result.

Symptoms: muscle and ligament injury gives rise to a sharp shooting pain in the neck, back of the head or shoulder, especially when the head is turned in a particular direction.

Treatment: a cold compress or ice-pack will ease the initial pain and help the inflammation settle. So too will a mild painkiller, such as aspirin or paracetamol. The neck must be rested for the first 24-48 hours, preferably in a soft surgical collar. Then gentle mobilising exercises can be started to avoid chronic stiffness. These can be combined with heat and massage to ease away muscle spasm.

Suspected Broken Neck

This can result from a fall on the head, whiplash injury or severe wrenching of the neck. If the fracture causes dislocation of the vertebrae, the spinal cord may be compressed. If this occurs high in the neck the vital brain stem is damaged and death results (as in judicial hanging). In rugby the lower vertebrae are more likely to be broken. Spinal cord compression at this level causes numbness and tingling in the trunk and limbs, and if severe, permanent paralysis of the arms and perhaps legs.

Symptoms: suspect spinal cord compression if the player cannot move his limbs or feels numbness or tingling in them.

Treatment: extreme care must be taken not to move the casualty until a properly trained ambulance crew arrive. If necessary, the game must be stopped. The slightest shift of the fractured neck vertebrae could increase the pressure on the spinal cord with dire consequences. Only skilled people should handle the casualty.

Shoulder

Heavy falls on the shoulder or outstretched arm, heavy tackling, and wrenched arm in the ruck can all cause shoulder injury, ranging from a pulled muscle or sprained ligament to a dislocated shoulder or broken collar-bone.

Strains and Sprains

Symptoms: a sharp pain when the arm is moved, usually in one particular direction. Pain from a pulled muscle or tendon is felt on active movement against resistance. Pain from a sprained ligament is felt on active or passive movement. With these injuries there may also be swelling or bruising.

Treatment: an ice-pack can bring immediate relief and help to prevent long-term stiffness. Gentle movement should be attempted, even in the early stages after injury, to prevent the development of a 'frozen shoulder'.

Dislocation

Symptoms: severe pain and loss of use of the arm. Dislocation also gives the shoulder a curiously angled appearance, as the arm bone has been forced out of joint.

Treatment: support arm in a sling or with other arm. Do not attempt to put the shoulder back unless you have been taught exactly how to. This should be done at the hospital accident department.

Broken Collar-bone

Either caused by a direct hard tackle or an indirect jarring from a fall on an outstretched arm.

Symptoms: pain, swelling and a rounded, fallen shoulder make the diagnosis obvious.

Treatment: support the arm in a makeshift sling, or with the other hand, and seek treatment at hospital.

Arms

Most often injured in the ruck and scrum and in tackles. Sprains and strains are the most likely injuries, and should be treated as per p. 81.

Wrist Fractures

These are not uncommon. Treatment advice is given on p. 87.

Fingers

Fingers frequently get bent backwards, trodden upon, or kicked as they handle the ball, causing sprains, dislocations and lacerations.

Treatment: ice and immobilisation are the key elements of treatment. One finger can be splinted against its neighbour. Lacerations require a clean dry dressing and may need stitches.

Trunk

The most common problems here are low back injury and broken ribs or sprung cartilages in the ribs – often caused by leg twisting in the tackles.

Fractured Ribs

Most often caused by a heavy tackle or direct kick.

Symptoms: severe pain on moving or coughing, and usually bruising.

Treatment: ice to reduce swelling and bruising. A mild analgesic such as aspirin or paracetamol to reduce pain. Any difficulty in breathing requires hospital attention.

Low Back Pain

Most commonly caused by muscular spasm either resulting from a strain or to protect a sprained ligament. Heavy falls, tackles and kicks can easily injure the lumbar region. Slipped discs are less likely but can occur when mauling opponents in the ruck.

Treatment: rest lying flat on a firm bed or the floor for at least 48 hours. Warmth and massage can ease the pain. Then begin gentle weight-bearing and mobilisation exercises.

Legs

The site of most rugby injuries. Pulled muscles, strained tendons, sprained ligaments and fractures, as well as the obvious catalogue of cuts, abrasions and bruises – mostly the result of kicks and being tripped.

Groin Strain

Caused by high-speed lateral movement of the leg. A classic situation in rugby is being tackled hard from one side whilst the weight is on the leg of that side. The inner thigh muscle is suddenly stretched and, unless adequately conditioned, is strained.

Treatment: cold compress or ice-pack for the first few hours. Then gentle exercises to stretch and strengthen the inner thigh muscle.

Pulled Hamstring

A fairly common injury mainly caused by sudden starts and sprints involving stretching of fairly unconditioned muscles at the back of the thigh.

Symptoms: usually a sharp pain is felt just above the knee at the back.

Treatment: a cold compress or ice-pack helps to relieve pain and inflammation. The important thing is to keep the leg moving gently from the second day onwards to avoid stiffening. Gentle hamstring-stretching exercises should be performed. After a severe hamstring pull, you can expect several weeks of rehabilitation before returning to play.

Torn Quads

This is a pulled quadriceps muscle at the front of the thigh. Usually the result of a blocked kick. Because of the bulk of the quads, tears in this muscle are usually only partial.

Treatment: along the same lines as for hamstring pulls. Initial rest and ice, followed next day by very gentle quads-stretching exercises to maintain full range of movement. Later quads-strengthening exercises can be started, but never to the point of pain. Again, think in terms of weeks rather than days for full recovery.

Knees

Knee sprains are common in rugby, hence so many bandages in action. Heavy tackling is the main culprit. A sideways tackle can sprain the side ligament of the weight-bearing knee. A tackle from the front can hyper-extend the knee, i.e. force it to bend backwards. The patella and patellar tendon can be damaged by a direct kick or forced flexion.

Symptoms: sprains are extremely painful and incapacitating. The knee may swell rapidly with fluid as the joint-lining responds to trauma.

Treatment: no attempt should be made to continue play. Ice-packs should be applied rapidly to reduce swelling and the knee strapped firmly in the locked-straight position. For the first 24-48 hours the leg should be rested and elevated, with repeated ice-packs. Then gentle mobilisation exercises should be started to maintain range of movement. Then knee-strengthening exercises (knee-straightening exercises against increasing

resistance), but never to the point of pain. Gradually build up walking, stair-climbing, cycling and jogging until you can do crouch jumps with ease.

Ankles

Sprained ankles are another common problem resulting from a stumble or tackle. The weight-bearing foot is violently wrenched sideways, spraining the side ligament of the ankle.

Symptoms: pain, swelling and perhaps bruising over the torn ligament are the usual symptoms. It is a mistake to carry on playing regardless and 'work it through'. The result will be more damage and longer incapacitation.

Treatment: immediate ice or cold spray, firm strapping and elevation. Repeated ice-packs for 24-48 hours, keeping the ankle rested and elevated as much as possible. Then gentle up and down movements of the ankle can be started to avoid stiffening. Then shin-strengthening exercises followed by bicycle work. Only when the pain and swelling have subsided should weight-bearing exercises be attempted.

Achilles Tendon

More a problem for half-backs and three-quarters when reaching low to catch the ball on the run.

Symptoms: Sudden sharp pain in the low calf, sometimes accompanied by a loud snap. The calf muscle may bunch up in an agonising knot.

Treatment: rest-ice-compression-elevation (The R-I-C-E routine) should be started immediately with cold spray and ice-packs, plus firm strapping. Complete rupture will need hospitalisation. For partial tears, repeated ice and elevation for 48 hours can be followed by gradual mobilisation consisting of gentle stretching of the calf, followed a few days later by calf-strengthening exercises.

Feet

Apart from ankle injuries, the feet are remarkably rarely injured in rugby. Most likely is a 'stress fracture' of one of the metatarsal bones in the forefoot, causing pain, swelling and bruising. An X-ray will show the fracture.

Treatment: R-I-C-E again. Firm strapping, ice-packs and elevation are usually the only treatment required. But the injury requires weeks off the field for full healing.

General Ailments and Conditions

It is also useful for sportsmen and women to know something about the more general ailments and conditions that are difficult to avoid, whatever their chosen sport.

Skin and Subcutaneous Tissue

The skin and subcutaneous tissues are most vulnerable to friction and impact.

Blisters

These are caused by repeated friction of unprotected skin in which the outer layer of skin (epidermis) is separated from the inner layer (dermis) by inflammatory tissue fluid – or occasionally blood (the blood blister).

Treatment: if the blister is not likely to cause trouble it can be left alone to settle, but if in danger of being rubbed, cover it with a piece of sticking plaster.

Usually, however, it is threatening to burst and this is the moment when infection can occur. On these occasions it is best to lance it under sterile conditions. First cleanse the skin thoroughly with antiseptic. Then sterilise a needle in a flame for a few seconds and holding it parallel to the skin puncture the edge of the blister (*do not remove the loose skin*). Gently dab dry and squeeze to remove the fluid, then cover with a porous sticking plaster.

Prevention: you can prevent blisters by using sticking plaster to cover any rubbing point that is beginning to feel sore. The first indications of a blister are likely to be a soreness and reddening of the area.

Abrasions (Grazes)

Abrasions are due to the scuffing away of the epidermis completely.

Treatment: cleanse under a running tap to wash away dirt or grit (or use an antiseptic solution). When thoroughly clean, allow wound to dry, or dry by dabbing with a sterile gauze, and cover with a porous dressing.

Minor Cuts

Minor cuts should be treated similarly and covered with a sticking plaster. For more severe lacerations and bleeding see First Aid, p. 83.

Deep, Penetrating Wounds

Deep, penetrating wounds, such as caused by a nail spiking the foot, may need a tetanus injection. If the wound has been made by an object which you suspect as being infected, you are advised as a matter of course to have a precautionary tetanus injection.

Bruises (Contusions)

Bruises are areas of skin and subcutaneous tissue in which the tiny capillaries are damaged by a sudden blow. (The colouring of a bruise is due to blood oozing into the tissue.)

Treatment: an ice-pack (ice cubes in a towel – it is a mistake to apply ice direct to the skin [see illustration]) applied as soon as possible to the bruise will help to reduce the colouring and swelling. However, if the blow was severe, bruising may mask a fracture of the underlying bone and an X-ray is advisable.

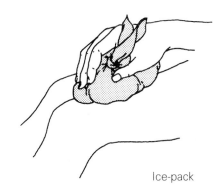

Ice-pack

Muscle Injuries

These are usually due to repeated over-use or sudden over-stretching of untuned muscles. Most can be prevented by adequate fitness and training, and the all-important warm-up before strenuous exercise.

Muscle Aches (Muscle Soreness, Stiffness)

Muscle aches are caused by imposing unaccustomed exercise on groups of untrained muscles.

When muscles are worked hard they will swell with tissue fluid from the capillaries surrounding the muscle fibres. The fluid bathes the fibres and carries away irritant waste products of muscle contraction. *Untrained* muscles remain swollen with fluid long after exercise has stopped and this causes pain and stiffness which can take place as much as 12-24 hours afterwards, although usually much sooner.

Treatment: muscle aches can be relieved by warmth to increase the blood flow (e.g. a hot bath, shower, hot-water bottle or embrocation.) Gentle massage and kneading the affected muscle may also help, especially while under hot water.

Muscle Spasm (Cramp)

Cramp is a sudden involuntary contraction of a muscle – classically the calf – causing temporary but crippling pain. It usually results from over-exertion, poor co-ordination or extreme cold – when the muscles tense – or extreme heat – when excessive sweating can lead to salt depletion.

Treatment: the most effective way to deal with cramp is to stretch the knotted muscle, in order to pull it out of spasm, and then massage it along its length.

Prevention: in hot weather add a pinch or two of salt to a fruit drink.

Stitch

A stitch is a spasm or cramp of a muscle in the side of the trunk, usually felt between or below the lower ribs.

Treatment: it can be eased by taking a deep breath in and holding it. Other techniques are to flex the trunk to the side away from the stitch or push the fingers deep into the side and bend forward.

Prevention: avoid exertion within two hours of a heavy meal.

Muscle Pulls or Tears

Muscle pulls or tears are the most common form of muscle injury and are caused by a muscle suddenly becoming over-stretched and rupturing some of the fibres. This causes intense pain, swelling and loss of function. A pulled muscle is often the result of a sudden awkward or unexpected movement in sport – a twist, or sudden stop or turn.

Treatment: stop immediately, for it is essential to rest the injured muscle as soon as possible (it would be agony to use it anyway). Apply an ice-pack and strap the pack to the injured muscle with a firm bandage in order to apply compression. If possible, elevate the injured part to help drain away inflammatory fluid.

This routine is the classic prescription for soft-tissue injuries and is sometimes given the shorthand name of R-I-C-E. (i.e. rest – ice – compression – elevation).

After 48 hours start gentle mobilisation exercises: flex the injured part back and forwards *gently*, taking care to avoid painful movement. It may also be useful to try alternate hot and cold treatments (hot towels/ice-packs alternating every 20-30 minutes). After a few days' passive stretching, you can begin active exercise, building up gradually to full activity in a few weeks.

Prevention: to avoid pulled or torn muscles it is essential to carry out a thorough warm-up before exercise (*see p. 27*).

Tendons

These are the tough fibrous strands on which muscles tug to flex or extend joints. Tendons are sometimes strained, partially torn or completely ruptured.

Symptoms: these range from pain and swelling to total loss of function.

Treatment: for lesser injuries the R-I-C-E routine (*see above*) should be started immediately; the cold compress reduces inflammation and damage. If the tendon is ruptured (and the muscles then bunch into a knot or spasm), medical attention should be sought.

Tendon Sheath

In some sports, over-use of a particular joint can lead to an irritation of the tendon sheath or lining. The resulting inflammation is called *tenosynovitis* (tendonitis) and causes shooting pain when the joint is moved.

Tendinous Insertions

Additionally, where the bulk of a muscle is anchored to a bone there are short tendinous insertions. These can sometimes be torn, usually when movement is suddenly blocked and the muscle is jarred (e.g. a squash player hitting the wall, a football player mis-kicking). The shin and elbow are classic sites of such tendinous insertions. When torn, this leads to 'shin splints' for the former and 'tennis elbow' for the latter.

Treatment: applying an ice-pack may give relief, but rest is the only cure. Your doctor may recommend other treatments and these may alleviate the symptoms temporarily, but the trouble will return unless the limb is rested because tendons are very slow to heal.

Sprains

Sprain is the term used to describe a partially torn ligament, which is a fibrous strap binding the bones of a joint together.

If a ligament tears, the joint cannot be moved without pain and soon swells. Classic sites are the ankle, the knee and the wrist.

Treatment: immediate course of action is the R-I-C-E routine. Rest is crucial; continued use of the joint will lead to chronic disability.

Bone Injuries (*see First Aid, p. 87*)

Hot-weather Ailments

Heat Exhaustion

Excessive sweating can lead to loss of essential water and salts. Usually, thirst provides a strong incentive to drink to replace the water, but not the salt. Salt depletion causes the victim to feel dizzy and faint, probably with a headache. It may also bring cramp (*see p. 80*). If salt is not replaced soon this can lead to the highly dangerous heat stroke (*see First Aid, p. 87*).

Prevention: add an extra pinch or two of salt to your food in hot weather before exercise.

Prickly Heat

Prickly heat is another hot-weather condition. It is caused by high humidity making the skin waterlogged, thus blocking the sweat glands and causing irritation.

Prevention: wear light, loose cotton-type clothing and try to restrict exertion to the cooler times of the day.

Sunburn

Prevention: use a suitable sunscreen to protect exposed parts.

Treatment: sunburn can be relieved with cool water or calamine lotion.

Cold-weather Ailments

Physical activity in cold weather usually keeps you warm, but the extremities – ears, nose, fingers and toes – can be affected by cold, when they will turn white and feel numb. In extreme conditions they can even become frostbitten. So wear suitable headgear, gloves and extra socks in very cold weather.

Also, in these conditions, muscles tend to tense up. So to avoid injury it is important to carry out a thorough warm-up routine before exertion (*see p.27*).

Prolonged exposure to severe cold, especially if soaked to the skin, can lead to the potentially fatal hypothermia.

First Aid for Sports

There are a number of common and not-so-common, sporting emergencies. This section discusses how to deal with them until medical help arrives. Most First Aid is simple practical common sense. But some techniques – in particular mouth-to-mouth respiration and cardiac massage – can really only be learned properly from a qualified instructor.

Bleeding

Severe bleeding is usually from a deep cut (laceration), torn flesh (avulsion) or penetrating wound.

Symptoms: spurting, bright-red blood indicates that an artery has been severed and the flow must be stopped *immediately*. Oozing darker blood from the veins indicates that the situation is not so urgent but the blood flow should be stopped as soon as possible.

Treatment: with both types of blood flow the treatment is essentially the same. With a clean handkerchief, or pad of absorbent material, or even your bare hands, hold together the edges of the wound and press hard to stop bleeding.
Maintaining the pressure, lay the casualty down and raise the injured part above the level of the heart, if possible. If blood seeps through the pad put another on top. *Do not release the pressure on the wound.*

Reassure the casualty and send for medical assistance, but do not leave the casualty alone for more than a minute or two, and only if you have bound the pressure pad in place.
Gaping wounds will usually need stitches. Deep wounds, especially those caused by a dirty or muddy object, may call for an anti-tetanus injection.

Nosebleed

Treatment: pinch the soft part of the nose for 10-15 minutes, or until bleeding stops. Do not swallow blood but spit it out into a cup or basin. Do not blow or pick the nose and try to avoid sneezing for the next 12 hours. An ice-pack over the nose will also prove beneficial.

Breathing Difficulty

Choking

Choking is unusual in sports, but may occur if someone inhales chewing gum or a false tooth. A blocked windpipe makes the person struggle for breath and the lips turn blue.

Treatment: get the casualty to bend forward and give him several sharp slaps between the shoulder blades to help dislodge the blockage. If this doesn't work, try the Heimlich Manoeuvre *(see illustrations)*. If you cannot clear the blockage quickly, send for urgent medical help; an emergency tracheotomy may be necessary.
Similarly, call for urgent medical help if someone is choking due to a sharp blow to the

throat which has caused internal swelling of the windpipe, or if someone has a severe attack of asthma.

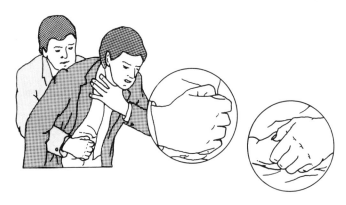

Heimlich Manoeuvre. Stand behind the casualty. Put your arm around his waist making a fist with one hand, clasping it with the other, and with thumbs resting just above his navel. Make three or four sharp pulls diagonally upwards towards you.

Stopped Breathing

If a person loses consciousness, perhaps after a blow to the head, or a faint, they may stop breathing and start to go purplish-blue. This may simply be because the tongue has fallen against the back of the throat and blocked the windpipe.

Treatment: turn the person face down so that the tongue can fall forwards. If he takes a long breath in and continues to breathe, keep him in this face down 'recovery' position (sometimes called the 'coma' position) and send for medical help (*see illustration*).

If no breath follows, then turn him face up again

and start mouth-to-mouth respiration (the 'kiss of life') (*see illustrations*).

Mouth-to-mouth Respiration: with one hand pinch his nostrils shut and push his forehead back so that his chin juts upwards. With the other hand hold his jaw open and lift it away from his neck to pull the tongue off the back of the throat. Now take a deep breath and, sealing your lips round the casualty's mouth, blow air into his lungs, watching to see his chest rise as you do so. Then remove your mouth and watch his chest fall again. Do this four times and then check the pulse (*see p.9*). If the heart is beating, continue mouth-to-mouth at the rate of 16-18 breaths a minute, checking the pulse every minute or so. If you are doing the job properly the casualty's lips and tongue should become a healthy-looking pink. Keep the respiration going until help arrives or until the casualty starts to breathe spontaneously, in which case turn him face down into the recovery position (*see illustration*).

If you cannot feel his pulse, or he remains purple despite several good respirations, then his heart has stopped beating, and you must start cardiac massage immediately (*see p.86*).

The recovery, or coma position

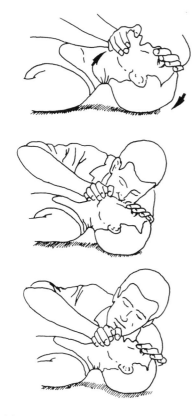

Mouth-to-mouth artificial respiration

Symptoms: the classic symptom of a heart attack is a heavy vice-like pain in the chest – like severe indigestion – which may spread to the arms or jaw. The victim usually feels faint and sick.

Treatment: if you suspect a heart attack, send someone for an ambulance, but do not leave the victim alone.

If he remains conscious, rest and reassurance are the most important things. Get him in a half-sitting position with his shoulders propped on a rolled up coat or blanket (*see illustration*). Loosen his clothing and cover him with a coat or towel. Do *not* give him anything by mouth, not even brandy or aspirin. Stay with him until help arrives.

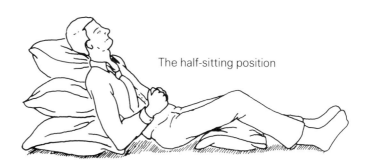

The half-sitting position

Heart Problems

Heart Attack

This is a not uncommon misfortune that may befall the unfit (usually men) who suddenly over-exert themselves. Most people survive their first heart attack, but smokers have double the risk of dying.

If he loses consciousness and stops breathing suspect cardiac arrest (stopped heart) which calls for immediate cardiac massage, and mouth-to-mouth respiration.

Stopped Heart (Cardiac Arrest)

This is to be suspected if a person collapses unconscious and stops breathing. The victim will probably go an ashen colour with purple lips and tongue. The cause may be a heart attack or severe attack following haemorrhage or crush injury.

Treatment: feel for the casualty's pulse. Put two fingers at *one side* of his Adam's apple and press firmly. If you cannot feel pulsations, try the other side. Look at the pupils of his eyes. No pulse and wide fixed pupils spells cardiac arrest. Start cardiac massage immediately. *This is not to be attempted if the heart is beating (see illustrations).*

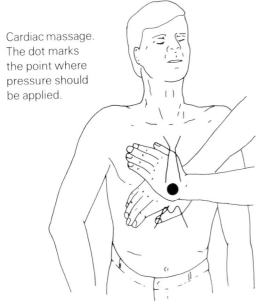

Cardiac massage. The dot marks the point where pressure should be applied.

Cardiac Massage: lay the person on his back on firm ground. Quickly clear his mouth of any vomit or blood clot with a sweep or two of your finger. Give four breaths of mouth-to-mouth respiration as above. This may be enough to stimulate the heart into action, so quickly check the heart again.

If there is still no pulse, kneel alongside the casualty. Put the heel of one hand on the lower half of his breast-bone in the midline, just above the V-shaped notch made by the ribs. Cover this hand with the heel of the other. Now keeping your arms straight, push down on your hands, moving his breastbone down about 6.25 cm (1½ in.) and release. Repeat this pressure about 80 times a minute. Count to yourself: one pressure, two pressure, three pressure . . . etc. After 15 pressures, give two more respirations, and then continue pressures. Keep going with 15 pressures, 2 respirations etc. Every few minutes stop to check the pulse. If you feel one, stop cardiac massage but continue respirations. If spontaneous breathing starts, put him in the recovery position (*see illustration*). Do not abandon your efforts until help arrives.

Unconsciousness

Usually caused by a blow to the head, but sometimes due to a diabetic coma, epileptic fit or heart attack (*see above*).

The most important action is to check for breathing. If the casualty is not breathing, mouth-to-mouth respiration must be started immediately.

If the casualty is unconscious but still breathing, turn him face down into the 'recovery' or 'coma' position (*see p. 84*). This allows the tongue to fall forwards away from the back of the throat where it would block the windpipe.

Send for immediate medical help, but do not leave the casualty unattended, check his breathing every few minutes.

Head Injury

This can range from a cut scalp to a fractured skull, but usually refers to a blow on the head sufficient to knock out the victim for seconds or minutes.

Concussion

The likely consequence is concussion, a temporary disorientation causd by jarring the brain. This may be accompanied by giddiness and memory loss.

Contusion (Bruising)

More serious is brain contusion, which leaves a scar in the brain substance and usually causes some permanent loss of memory and intellectual capacity (i.e. 'punch-drunk').

Compression

The most serious and life-threatening result is compression: an inter-cranial haemorrhage (bleeding inside the skull). The build-up of pressure can rapidly lead to loss of consciousness and death, unless the pressure is released by emergency surgery. Compression can occur up to 48 hours after injury.

Symptoms: drowsiness, confusion, dilation of one or both pupils of the eye.

Treatment: any person knocked out by a head injury should be made to lie quietly and be looked at every half hour or so to check the level of consciousness.

If you observe any of the symptoms of compression listed above, get the victim to hospital immediately.

Facial Injury

Black Eye

Usually looks far worse than it is. As soon as you can, apply an ice-pack or cold compress to prevent or reduce the swelling. It is wise to have the eye checked by a doctor to make sure that vision is not impared.

Broken Nose

Usually accompanied by bleeding, swelling and deformed appearance. Bleeding should be stopped as described above (*p. 83*). Sometimes the nose can be straightened immediately, but usually it is best to put on an ice-pack or cold compress and get the casualty to hospital.

Broken cheekbones and broken jaws should also be covered with an ice-pack to reduce swelling and the casualty taken to hospital.

Fractures and Dislocations

Broken bones and disrupted joints are usually obvious, especially in the more serious cases. Sometimes, however, swelling and bruising can mask such injuries, e.g. stress fracture of the foot.

Treatment: it is important not to try to bear weight on a fracture or dislocation as this could damage a nerve or blood vessel. It is also important not to try to straighten the injury, unless you know precisely what you are doing, for you could cause even more damage.

The most useful thing to do is to keep the injured part as immobile as possible – use splints, slings or stretchers as necessary. The casualty should be taken to hospital where the injury can be X-rayed and the deformity reduced under medical supervision, with an anaesthetic if necessary.

Treatment: numbed and frozen extremities should be got into the warm as soon as possible and held against warm skin. *Do not apply direct heat and do not rub the frozen part* – you might literally rub the flesh away. Do not stand or walk on frozen toes or feet, but rest with the feet up.

Environmental Emergencies

Heat Stroke

This is a very serious condition and can occur after prolonged exertion in a very hot or humid environment. It is caused by the body's temperature-regulating system breaking down and, as a result, the temperature rises alarmingly.

Symptoms: the victim has a hot dry skin, rapid pulse and looks flushed. Confusion and coma can follow rapidly.

Treatment: *medical attention is urgent.* The important thing is to *cool* the victim down as quickly as possible with water or ice, and then to keep him fanned to induce cooling.

Frostbite

This is also potentially serious. The body is composed of 70 per cent water and if ice-crystals form in human tissue it is destroyed.

Index